SUSSEX
FOLK

The Folk Song Revival in Sussex

Clive Bennett

COUNTRY BOOKS

First published in 2002 by Country Books,
Courtyard Cottage, Little Longstone, Bakewell,
Derbyshire DE45 INN, England
in conjunction with Clive Bennett

ISBN I 898941 78 5

Printed by:
MFP Design & Print

CONTENTS

DEDICATION

This book is dedicated to all the people who have visited folk song clubs during the past 40 years. Within these pages are the details of clubs, singers and organisers involved in maintaining the folk song tradition of Sussex in and around Brighton. Without the support of the thousands of enthusiasts who attended these events however the story would have been very different.

ACKNOWLEDGEMENTS

I could not have written this book without the generous help of many people who kindly allowed me to reproduce photographs from their personal collections and supplied much additional information. Notably these included: Roger Brasier, John Collyer, Sandra Goddard, Mrs R Harvey, Pat Howell, Tim Kent, Terry Masterson, Brian Matthews, Bob McDonald, Mary Norsworthy, Sylvia Parsons, Ron Pope, Brian Shuel [Collections], Vic and Tina Smith, George Wagstaff, Tony Wales, Jim Ward, Miles Wootton and Mike Yates. My particular thanks go to Jim Marshall for a wealth of information arising from an early draft of the book and the bulk of the photographs. A special mention for my partner Cherie Davies who for several years has endured stacks of magazines, scrapbooks, newspaper cuttings and photographs scattered around the home and my hours of late night work on the computer.

FOREWORD

This book is a real labour of love that shows Clive Bennett's devotion to his subject. It's an almost unbelievably detailed and fascinating account of the past forty years of folk music clubs in Sussex – and what memories it evokes! It tells of the comings and goings of venues and singers, and is a virtual Who's Who of performers. We are fortunate that in our county we had – and thankfully still have – some of the finest traditional singers in England, and the pages devoted to them at the end of the book are a pleasure to read. It is heart-warming that the scene is still flourishing so strongly here in Sussex, and the credit for this must go to the organisers and the floor singers of the clubs. It is their hard work, their passion and their time, always freely given, that keeps the clubs alive.

     Thanks, Clive. Thanks all.

          Shirley Collins, Hove 2001

1 THE FIRST CLUBS

The reawakening of popular interest in British traditional song, more commonly referred to as the folk revival, reached Brighton in the summer of 1961, soon after the early wave of blues based skiffle guitarists discovered first American and then British folk songs.

Nationally Brighton was, and remains, unusual and possibly unique in the way the early organisers of folk clubs quickly colonised the surrounding area with a series of similar clubs in nearby towns, first Worthing then Shoreham, followed soon after by Eastbourne and lastly its nearest neighbour, Lewes. Its sphere of influence became the most widespread and significant in the county and endured for forty years. Today the precise reason for this development based on Brighton is not immediately obvious since elsewhere in Sussex as in most parts of the country individual clubs eventually developed, which were almost invariably independent from what was happening in the surrounding area.

Back in the early nineteen sixties however its location at the hub of the local railway system made Brighton the natural focal point for all forms of entertainment, attracting young people from towns and villages as far away as Littlehampton in the west, Crawley to the north and Eastbourne in the east. This was a time before the modern consumer society achieved the status of virtually every family having at least one car and the teenagers and those in their early twenties were individually generally far less mobile than today's youth. They were used to relying on public transport and particularly the extensive railway network that was then in existence. The main form of entertainment was the cinema and while almost every town possessed at least one Brighton had nine, with four more in Hove. There were also more dance halls and even nightclubs, which were rare in other locations and in addition Brighton possessed a popular ice rink.

It may well be that its size and cosmopolitan nature coupled with this regular influx of young people were significant in creating a suitable arena for the development of what was, at first, very much a minority interest form of entertainment.

In considering the development of folk clubs in Brighton while individual motives for running a folk session varied one thing all the organisers of the early clubs in the town clearly had in common was a pioneering spirit. Not only were there no other clubs in the area but also very few in the country for them to use as role models.

Within a short space of time however, during the early 1960's, the 'folk boom' developed creating a demand for similar clubs in nearby towns. Encouraged by the enthusiasts who had been commuting to Brighton to experience this 'new' form of music the organisers of the first Brighton clubs were willing to respond since they had already acquired both the experience and contacts to open new ventures outside the central conurbation. These key individuals involved with this early development subsequently proved to be very dedicated to the genre and most remained involved with folk song and club organising for 30 years or more which helped ensure that several of the early clubs were extremely long running ventures. This is perhaps even more remarkable when you realise that they all quickly learnt that there was no great commercial gain from running a folk club.

This book seeks to highlight what appears to be a local phenomenon, identifying the individuals involved and the major clubs they founded while also documenting the general evolution of folk song clubs in Brighton and the relationships they had with clubs in the surrounding towns.

It is perhaps worthwhile noting that virtually none of the central figures with long term involvement either in running song clubs in the town or the expansion into the surrounding towns was born in the area. Few, in fact, were actually born in Sussex.

SINGING ACROSS THE COUNTY

Historically the singing and playing of traditional songs and music has a long and distinguished pedigree in Sussex. This has persisted well into the twentieth century with performers of the calibre of The Coppers from Rottingdean, George 'Pop' Maynard of Copthorne, Scan Tester from Horsted Keynes, George Townshend from Lewes, George Belton of Madehurst, Bob Blake in Broadbridge Heath and George and Ron Spicer from Turners Hill.

George 'Pop' Maynard
Brian Matthews

It would seem therefore natural, almost inevitable, that the county should be straddled with the network of revival song clubs that are enjoyed by so many folk enthusiasts today, but it wasn't always like that. At the start of the 1960's there were just three formal folk song clubs in the whole of the county which were located in Horsham, Hastings and East Preston, near Littlehampton. While the East Preston club lasted only a few weeks both Horsham and Hastings evolved into long running clubs, whose successors are still extant today, although not without a number of changes along the way.

Beyond the Brighton area already mentioned, other clubs were eventually born but in many cases this evolution took another decade. At the western extremity of the county, in Chichester, folk song arrived on 7 January 1962 with informal singarounds in the Wagon and Horses, although this was preceded in the early 60's by the thriving Martlett Morris Men and the local folk dance club. The first formal song club was organised on Sunday evenings at the White Horse in February 1963 by Paul Morris, an engineer and art designer who lectured at Brighton Art College by day and in his spare time was a Morris dancer who also sang and played the guitar. At the time of his early death at the age of 36 in 1970 in a go-kart accident Paul was senior lecturer at the Ulster College of Art. The club itself, despite changes of name and venue, continues until this day now meeting at the Gribble Inn, Oving, near Chichester having recently changed from Friday to Tuesday evenings. Still in the far west of the county Amberley folk club opened in July 1972 but after eight years became a monthly meeting before closing in 1993, while in Arundel, The Willows Folk Club opened in 1973 at the cricket club and is, like Chichester, still running today – although it underwent a number of changes following the death of founder Bill Hedges in 1993, including closing for several months early in 1998. A little later, from 1974 there was a regular folk club in Bognor Regis but this closed after seven years.

Not until Tuesday 4 January 1972 did Crawley have its first folk song club and even then it was in Three Bridges where it met at the Locomotive. This club survived various moves, from the Locomotive to the Apple Tree in Crawley, on to the Leisure Centre, the Bewbush Centre, the Plough at Three Bridges, the Plough at Rusper and finally the Red Lion at Turners Hill. It also changed days several times from Tuesday to Sunday to Saturday and in 1999 to Friday. A few months after the Crawley club first appeared a club was opened in Haywards Heath meeting fortnightly from 13 August 1972 at the Fox with Chris Gutteridge and Derek Lockwood as residents and Johnie Winch as the first guest. The club survived for five years, closing in August 1977, by which time it was being organised by Linda Armstrong. Nearby a club opened in Burgess Hill, meeting on Thursday evenings in the Junction Inn from November 1978 until June 1979 under the guidance of Dick Richardson and Lynn Clayton.

But these were all later. To begin we return to the Sussex scene of 1960.

Horsham

Horsham Songswappers' met monthly on Wednesday evenings in the Albion (church) Hall. Founded in 1958 by Tony Wales there were no 'guest' singers as such but a fairly informal meeting of largely local people interested in folk music with tea and biscuits served during the interval.

The first meeting was on 30 March and over the next few years it included as regulars, among others, George Belton – where incidentally he introduced "The Sussex Toast" which is now so popular with many Sussex singers - Bob Blake, Harry Mousdell and Terry Potter with occasional visits from Scan Tester and Bill Agate. Tony, aided by members of this club, also conceived and organised one of the first folk festivals not only in Sussex but also in the country, which was held on Saturday 29 July 1961 at Horsham Boys Club, Hurst Road.

From lunchtime until midnight there was a non-stop singaround with the afternoon session compèred by Lionel Bounton and the evening by Geoff Rose. This was preceded on the Friday evening with a song and dance session in the Boys Club in Hurst Road for which Tony 'borrowed', for the first time in Sussex, the Celtic word "Ceilidh" which is now so common for such gatherings all over the country. Performers at that first festival included a host of traditional musicians and singers with Bob Blake, William 'Bill' Agate, Cyril Phillips, George Belton, George Townshend and Scan Tester.

Tony Wales [left] recording "Sussex Folk Songs and Ballads" in 1957 for Folkways Records. Accompanied on guitar by Peter Baxter.
'Bill' Agate [right] at Horsham Festival 1962
Tony Wales

There were also a number of the new generation of guitar playing singers three of whom, Geoff and Shirley Rose and Dick Richardson, were soon to feature in the development of the Brighton club scene. Another singer featured was Harry Mousdell who remains active in both folk song and Morris dancing around Horsham up to the present day.

1962 The author, Valerie Greenfield and Terry Scarlett at Horsham Folk Festival
the author

Horsham had been the home of Henry Burstow, rated by collector Ken Stubbs as the greatest traditional singer 'discovered' prior to the 1914-18 war and there was a display devoted to him at the festival. The festival was repeated in 1962 when the two sessions were 'chaired' by Harry Mousdell in the afternoon and Peter Kennedy in the evening. In 1963 there was a third festival but this time in the Albion Hall, subsequently demolished as part of the town centre re-development.

Tony Wales was at that time employed by the English Folk Dance and Song Society in London as Press and Publications Officer and Editor of English Dance and Song, the society's magazine, he was also responsible for the folk shop at Cecil Sharp House. In his spare time he had recorded an LP of traditional songs for the American Folkways label "Sussex Folk Songs and Ballads" [FG3515] and together with Terry Potter made a number of field recordings of traditional performers. He subsequently wrote several books on Sussex traditions and songs.

Tony has a unique place in the folk song revival in Sussex in that he was the first person to organise a regular weekly club in the county with the specific aim of furthering interest and knowledge of English traditional song and music.

Interest in folk song has, with varying degrees of success, persisted within the Horsham area right through until today [2002]. In 1964 Tony handed the running of the Songswappers club over to Terry Potter and the meetings transferred to the Citizens Advice Bureau in Queens Street where it remained until closing around 1966. There was then a break before Dave Toye opened a formal club in July 1969 meeting on Sunday evenings initially at the Station Hotel in Station Street before moving first, around October

1970, to the Swan Inn, West Street and then to The Anchor, East Street on 3 September 1972 where it remained until April 1976. By then the residents were Harry Mousdell – from the earlier Horsham Songswappers, Brian Blanchard, Dick Richardson, Simon Furey and Joan Crawley.

```
HORSHAM FOLK MUSIC FESTIVAL.   SATURDAY.JULY 29th 1961.

HORSHAM BOYS CLUB, HURST ROAD, HORSHAM.  3.0pm and 7.0pm.

Admission 2/- to either session.(3/6d combined admission
to both sessions). Performers admitted free to both sessions.

M.C. at 3.0pm Session.      LIONEL BOUNTON.
M.C. at 7.0pm Session.      GEOFF ROSE.

THE FOLLOWING HOPE TO TAKE PART.(Because this programme has
been prepared about ten days before the Festival,there
may be omissions and additions.)

CHANCTONBURY RING MORRIS MEN TEAM.
GEOFFREY COHEN (Haywards Heath) Scottish songs and
            Mouth Music.
JIM HOARE.(Shoreham) Violin.
WILLIAM AGATE (Rusper) Mouthorgan and Tambourine.
            MILES ATTERON (Redhill) Tyneside songs.
THE MERRYDOWNERS FOLK DANCE BAND (Horsham)
CHARLES REID.(Epsom) Bothy ballads.
TERRY POTTER (Horsham) Songs with guitar, Mouthorgan.
BASIL FELTON (Crawley) Guitar.
DEREK SMITH (Horsham) Piano Accordion.
DICK HOCK (Merstham) Songs with guitar.
J.NESTOR (Firle) Concertina.
GEORGE LAW (Glasgow) Songs with guitar.
C.A.PHILLIPS (Firle) Songs.
HORSHAM SQUARE DANCE CLUB TEAM.
SHEILA DOVE (Horsham) Songs.
GEORGE BELTON (Arundel) Traditional Singer.
HAYWARDS HEATH SCOTTISH FOLK DANCE CLUB group.
GEORGE TOWNSEND (Lewes) Traditional Singer.
MARY BARRON. (Arundel) Songs. Violin.
ARTHUR PEARSALL (Horsham) Songs with guitar.
HORSHAM JUNIOR THEATRE CLUB DANCE GROUP.
MRS ROLT (Fittleworth) Piano Accordion.
DICK RICHARDSON.(Redhill) Songs with guitar.
LIONEL BOUNTON (Horsham) Songs with guitar.
GEOFFREY AND SHIRLEY ROSE (Burgess Hill) Songs with banjo.
THE HIGHWAYMEN (Guildford) Folk Song group.
GEORGE "POP" MAYNARD (Copthorn) Traditional singer.
HARRY MOUSDELL (Horsham) Folk stories.
BOB BLAKE (Shipley) Traditional singer.

    REFRESHMENTS BETWEEN 5.30 and 7.0pm.

There will be a display devoted to Horsham Folk Singer
            HENRY BURSTOW.
There will also be a wide range of folk song and dance books
on sale during the afternoon and evening.
```

Horsham Festival Programme – 1961. *the author*

After this, from 13 March 1977 to 5 August 1979, there was a 'Horsham Folk Club' on alternate Sunday evenings in The Queens Head. By April 1987 it was again running, but at The Nelson, Trafalgar Road on the first and third Sundays each month until June 1993 then, after a summer break, as a weekly club from 5 September '93 until 1998. Then after briefly meeting at The Queens Head it transferred to the Horsham Cricket Club.

Hastings

Hastings, as an old fishing town, has many links with the sea and is still famed for its unique old net shops, tall tarred weatherboard buildings standing at the top of the beach known as the Stade at the eastern end of the town, just beyond the Lord Nelson. It also has a history of folk song and lore particularly among the fishing fraternity and it was here in the mid 1950's that Bob Copper, when collecting for the BBC, encountered Ned 'Wintry' Adams from whom he gathered a superb version of "The Bold Princess Royal".

Mary Norsworthy
[née Apps]
Mrs. Mary Norsworthy

The first folk song club however dates from 1960 when meetings started every Sunday in the Lord Nelson. This club was founded by John Freshwater who, within a few weeks, handed the organising over to Mary Apps (now Mrs. Norsworthy) who had become interested in folk music whilst attending Brighton Art College in the mid 1950's.

The club operated a policy of regular guest singers and those featured included Martin Carthy, The Strawberry Hill Boys, Julie Felix and the duo Joy Hyman and Martin Bell. Regular floor singers included a fine singer Johnny Sanderson from a gypsy family, Brian Hawes, Ted Bishop, Geoff Coates who accompanied Mary on guitar and featured with her on the television talent show "Home Grown" and Roy Nash, who today lives in Steyning where he organises a sing-around club meeting twice a month.

In the mid 1960's the club transferred, briefly, to the New Inn at Sidley and then, under the guidance of Colin Potter, to the Black Horse at Telham where the organising soon passed to Mick Marchant and John Goldsmith, a duo known collectively as 'Cottage'. Meanwhile a singaround session had started at the Three Oakes, Guestling hosted by 'The Mariners', a group consisting of Ted Bishop, one of the early regular floor singers at the Lord Nelson, Arthur Harmer, Michael Verral and John Towner. At the invitation of Mick and John of 'Cottage' John Towner and 'The Mariners' transferred to the Black Horse and took over the running of what was to become one of the best known and longest running folk clubs in the county.

Mary although now living in London remained involved with Sussex folk and as recently as 1993 was engaged in organising folk entertainment at Michelham Priory.

East Preston

Advertised simply as *'FOLK Ballads and Blues'* this club met every Wednesday in the Chequered Flag Club, a private member licensed club next to the then Blue Star (now Texaco) garage, adjacent to a roundabout on the A259 at Angmering. It was organised by Terry Scarlett of Rustington and myself – then living in East Preston – in the name of The Southern Folk Music Society and was our first attempt at promoting folk and jazz.

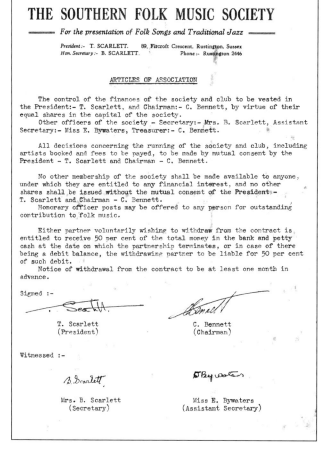

'Articles of Association' setting up The Southern Folk Music Society 1961

The author

The Southern Folk Music Society was initially Terry's idea, both to further his own part time career as a cabaret 'folk' entertainer – he had appeared on television on "Home Grown" and through that been taken up by a local agent with work at various venues during the evenings including a season at a club in Middleton near Bognor Regis – and to develop the promotion of folk song and traditional jazz as an entrepreneurial venture.

To develop this he invited me to join him in a commercial partnership, with an equal share of capital investment and the 'Society' was formed at a meeting on 20 April 1961. Terry's reasoning behind this arrangement was that people would pay a membership fee to join the club – but not the parent Society – and in return would be given reduced admission, priority bookings for concerts and possibly a newsletter which, it was hoped, would create a sense of being part of an organisation and encourage regular attendance. Since they were not however a member of the Society they would not have any involvement with the financial affairs of the club.

THE SOUTHERN FOLK MUSIC SOCIETY

FOLK

Ballads and Blues

at

THE CHEQUERD FLAG CLUB

every

WEDNESDAY 7-30 - 10-30 p.m.

Membership 5/- half year

Weekly Subscription 1/6   -   -   -   Guests 2/6

Guest Folk Singers and Musicians Especially Welcome

Licensed Bar ... . **Refreshments**

The Club adjoins THE BLUE STAR GARAGE

100 yards from Angmering Station — Bus Route 31 and 9

Southern Folk Music club poster.
The author

The sessions at the Chequered Flag Club commenced two weeks later on 3 May 1961 with Terry, Tony Atkinson and myself as residents, there were no guest performers instead it aimed, rather unsuccessfully, at attracting local singers but closed after ten weeks on 12 July. However, after closing this club Terry and I were soon to become involved in founding the Brighton folk scene.

Neither Terry nor I were natives of Sussex but we had both developed an interest in folk during the skiffle movement of the late 50's although from different backgrounds. Terry was from an urban environment and had recently moved to Sussex from London where he regularly visited the coffee bar folk sessions in the West End and had acquired a love for the Carter family style of American country music. I on the other hand had grown up in a small agricultural community in East Anglia before moving to Sussex in 1952. My interest was in the rural blues, stemming first from seeing the legendary American blues singer Big Bill Broonzy who had featured in a Chris Barber jazz concert at The Dome, Brighton and then from my involvement with 'The Mermaid', a floating coffee bar and hotel, moored on the river Arun at Littlehampton, which had been a focal point for jazz and guitar enthusiasts.

These three clubs embraced the two major styles of club organisation, which has survived to this day. The Horsham meetings were singaround and song swap sessions where everybody sat in a circle and each person in turn was afforded the opportunity to sing and, given the background of the regular performers at these sessions, it was natural that it would be structured largely around traditional English folk song.

The Hastings and East Preston sessions were more broad based including American folk songs and blues and both ran to a more formal pattern with a focal point from which anyone invited to sing, performed to the audience.

The emphasis at all three sessions was on audience participation and each featured a large number of chorus songs. With this in mind at East Preston Terry and I had settled on a policy of a club 'signature tune' which was used to open every session and with which everyone would be familiar and so enabling them to join in from the opening song of the day.

Early in July 1961 Malcolm Nixon, who ran an entertainment agency in London and represented, among others, Robin Hall, Jimmie McGregor, Steve Benbow and Long John Baldry, sent out a general invitation for folk club organisers around the country to attend a meeting at his office in Soho. On 13 July, the day after we closed the Chequered Flag Club, Terry and I, together with a small number of other folk club organisers, met Malcolm in London when he outlined his idea of a network of folk clubs in major centres which would provide work for the artistes he represented. Encouraged by his enthusiasm and offers to supply top singers at reasonable fees we agreed to open a folk song club in Brighton which was, Malcolm stressed, the key centre for the south coast.

One of the objectives was to attract a more middle of the road audience than the 'beatnik', or 'great unwashed' as some parts of the media called them, who were generally associated with what was still a musical revolution. This was the era when coffee bars presenting live music were fashionable with teenagers and very few folk clubs existed anywhere in the country. Certainly many of the audience they were seeking to attract were unlikely to frequent pubs on a regular basis.

But the seeds of the folk revival in Brighton and the creation of its first folk club had been planted by a would be entertainment impresario based in London. What evolved was one of the finest and most enduring folk scenes in the country that survived the ups and downs of changing public taste for almost forty years.

SINGING IN BRIGHTON

Brighton, like many towns, experienced an upsurge of interest among teenagers in creating music that typified the skiffle era. Two notable performers were Brian Matthews and Denis Grier who had been friends since their schooldays. Around 1957 they formed the 'Shingletown Skiffle Group' and on Saturday evenings ran a typical skiffle cellar club in the basement of the Queens Park Road Café in Egremont Place near Queens Park and it was here that a young novice guitarist Johnie Winch started to perform in public.

Brighton Skiffle Club poster 1957. *Maurice Funnell*

Saturday 8.oo - ll.oop.m.

SKIFFLE

AT

Brightons First

SKIFFLE CLUB

under

QUEENS PARK ROAD CAFE, EGREMONT PLACE.

with

BRIGHTONS MOST POPULAR GROUP

"THE SHINGLETOWN SKIFFLERS"

PLUS ATMOSPHERE

Trolley Buses **41** & **42** from Old Steine to the door

ONE YEARS FREE MEMBERSHIP FIRST NIGHT !

The room was small and inevitably led to the club closing in a relatively short time when it fell foul of fire regulations. At that time transport to Queens Park from the town centre was still by trolley bus.

As skiffle moved more towards commercialisation Brian, then in his mid 20's having been born in Brighton in 1937, found himself drawn the other way towards English traditional material. As a result he started visiting country pubs; The Punch Bowl at Turners Hill, Oak Tree, Ardingly and the Cherry Tree, Copthorne where he collected songs from source singers including George Spicer, George 'Pop' Maynard, Jim Wilson and Harry Holman. He also met the collector Ken Stubbs who told him about George Townshend who he subsequently visited at his home in Garden Street, Lewes. The recordings he made whilst visiting George in 1960 became the basis of a CD released by Musical Traditions forty years later.

The Ballad Tree Coffee Bar, King Street

Sometime around the middle of 1959 Brian and Denis approached Brighton Council and rented from it a former café in King Street, just off North Street, with the idea of converting the premises into a coffee bar and venue for home made music. They spent several days puzzling over a suitable name for their venture and then, by chance, Brian, who was reading The Ballad Tree, a study of British and American ballads by Evelyn Kendrick Wells, placed the book down on a table in front of Denis. Denis looked at the title and together they realised it was the perfect name for their new business and so was born The Ballad Tree Coffee Bar.

Brian Matthews *Brian Matthews*

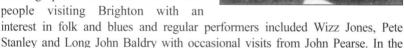

Normal opening hours were 11.00am to midnight and it rapidly became a favourite weekend haunt of what the local papers dubbed 'Beachniks' relating to the habit of weekend visitors from London sleeping out on the beach or under the piers. Of these 'beatniks' with bedrolls and guitars and the local art student population, anyone wishing to play or sing was allowed to do so. As a consequence it became the meeting place for both locals and people visiting Brighton with an interest in folk and blues and regular performers included Wizz Jones, Pete Stanley and Long John Baldry with occasional visits from John Pearse. In the evenings they would move along the road to the local pub, The Running Horse and then rush back to the Ballad Tree for a late night session at closing time. It was here, in September 1960 that I first experienced the emerging interest in British folk music.

Johnie Winch 1961 *The author*

The demise of this popular venue was however sudden and unpredictable. In the early summer of 1961 Brian was forced to enter hospital for an operation whilst at the same time Denis was pursuing amorous interests in Germany where he subsequently married and settled down. With both owners absent Lou Kinder was managing the coffee bar and, as Brian recalls, he over extended the premises credit limit. I remember singing there on Saturday 15 July but going back the following afternoon to find a group of thirsty would be singers waiting outside a locked and never to reopen building.

Brighton's next experience of folk was in 1960 when American singer

Ramblin' Jack Elliott appeared at the Co-op Hall, London Road in a concert sponsored by The People's Bookshop. The town's introduction to the folk revival as an organised art form for individual participation came however with an informal singaround which started in the early summer of 1961.

The Eagle, Gloucester Road

At about the time The Ballad Tree closed, Jack Perkins from The People's Bookshop in Gloucester Road, who was also secretary of the local branch of the Communist Party, started an informal session every Thursday evening in the upstairs room of The Eagle. People gathered to either listen to or join in a singaround/songswap session. Material ranged from Negro blues – where one of the most popular performers was the young but by then accomplished guitarist/singer Johnie Winch – through to unaccompanied English songs – where the accepted leading exponent was Brian Matthews and I remember hearing both perform there in September 1961.

No guest singers were used and admission was free but a hat was passed round to collect money to pay for the room. Within the modern definition of folk club, this informal weekly meeting could be argued as Brighton's first folk club but at the time 'folk club' implied something more formal.

The First Formal Clubs

Meanwhile Terry Scarlett and I, after much searching across the centre of Brighton for suitable venues for both an opening concert and regular weekly club meetings, had a further meeting in London on 12 August with Malcolm Nixon. Then on Sunday 17 September 1961 we presented a concert at The Co-op Hall, [now the Citygate Centre] London Road, again in the name of The Southern Folk Music Society, featuring The Galliards – at that time the top folk group in the country – comprising Robin Hall, Jimmie McGregor, Leon Rosselson and Shirley Bland.

Southern Folk Music Society concert poster. *The author*

Supporting performers were Gerry Loughran [Lockran as he was later known] a young blues singer from the Surbiton Folk Club making his

19

professional début and The Mariners – a group comprising Geoff and Shirley Rose, Dick Richardson and Dick Hook based on Reigate, which Terry and I had heard earlier in the year at the Horsham Folk Festival.

The concert was held in the evening but drew only a modest audience of about 100, however it heralded the opening of the **'Brighton Ballads and Blues Club'** which commenced regular weekly meetings the following Sunday afternoon, 24 September, from 3.00 to 6.00pm with blues singer Long John Baldry as the first guest.

Robin Hall, Shirley Bland, Jimmie MacGregor and Leon Rosselson. *The author*

The meetings were held in The Hideout Ballroom, on the second floor, above a coffee bar in East Street (part of the then ABC Savoy, later Canon cinema complex). This was **Brighton's first formal folk song club** and had a stated policy of bringing the top national performers of the day to Brighton. The 'signature' tune used by us to open each session for the first seven months and consequently the first song sung at Brighton's first folk club was "Foggy mountain top".

Membership at 1/= [5p] per annum rose rapidly to over two hundred and each week 80 to 90 people paying 2/6 [12.5p] each admission gathered to hear the residents, Terry Scarlett, Geoff and Shirley Rose from Burgess Hill [members of The Mariners who appeared at the opening concert] and myself together with any other local singers present, performing 'floor spots' of two or three songs in support of the week's professional guest – a format that was adopted by virtually all subsequent Brighton folk clubs.

Regular local singers included 'Whispering' Bob McDonald, a duo – Pat Howell and Bernie Cottam, Garry Farr – son of the famous boxer Tommy Farr, Johnie Winch – who, after a period as resident at later clubs in Brighton, turned professional and toured Britain and Europe and Pete '97' Hill – who frequently sang a music hall song with the improbable chorus of

"Gaily the troubadour waltzed around the waterbutt,
Crying my own love, come, come to me.
Gently a brickbat dropped upon his coconut,
The old man was watching from the old pear tree."

The Southern Folk Music Society

PRESENT

FOLK

at the Brighton Ballads & Blues Club

THE HIDEOUT BALLROOM, 70 EAST STREET, BRIGHTON

(Above A.B.C. SAVOY CINEMA)

Every SUNDAY 3 to 6 p.m.

Regular Appearance of LONDON ARTISTS

(Affiliated to the B.B.A.)

Membership 2/6

Enquiries: T. SCARLETT :: 89 FIRCROFT CRESCENT :: RUSTINGTON :: SUSSEX

Brighton Ballads and Blues Club poster *[left]. The author*

Terry Scarlett and the author *[above]* **performing at The Brighton Ballads and Blues Club in The Hideout Ballroom 24 September 1961.** *The author*

Amongst the first members on the opening day were Rod Machling, who later started singing and became resident at other Brighton clubs and Jim Marshall, who was to emerge as a major link in the development of the local folk scene when he later became organiser of Brighton's Sunday Folk Club, co founder BBC Radio Sussex's Minstrel Gallery and the Brighton/Sussex, Folk Diary.

Pete Hill and friend. *The author*

Other guest singers in the first three months included Steve Benbow, Derek Sarjeant and a new five-piece group from the north – The Liverpool Spinners whom, in addition to Tony Davis, Mick Groves, Hughie Jones and Cliff Hall, included Jacquie McDonald as female lead singer.

Liverpool Spinners at Brighton Ballads and Blues Club. 3 December 1961. Cliff Hall, Hughie Jones, Jacquie MacDonald, Tony Davis and Mick Groves. *The author*

Their appearance was the result of a conversation at the second meeting of the club when Joan Davis, a student on a weekend visit to the south coast, performed a floor spot and afterwards approached me about a booking for her brother's group with whom she had been singing before going to university. Another female vocalist had she added, taken her place. She went on to explain that they were not full time professionals but made regular visits to London from Liverpool at weekends to sing in the capital's folk clubs and she thought they would be able to travel to Brighton for a Sunday afternoon before returning home. We were not too sure but decided to give them a booking for the princely sum of £5 [£1 each] and so it was that on 22 October 1961 the Liverpool Spinners made their first of many trips to Brighton.

The Spinners made a return visit on 3 December 1961 but were then billed as "One of England's top folk groups" and the fee was doubled to £10. They did however bring the folk journalist/singer Eric Winter with them 'for the ride'. Virtually all of their numerous subsequent visits to the town were to be for sell out concerts at The Dome.

In October Terry and I received an irresistible offer from Tony Wales who

through his contacts as Press Officer for The EFDSS had been asked if he knew anyone who would organise a concert in the south of England for the legendary American folk singer Pete Seeger.

Pete Seeger *[left]. The author*

Pete was then on a world tour whilst on bail in the USA for un-American activities. With a sell out concert at The Royal Albert Hall, London, scheduled for the 16 November he wanted a smaller concert the night before as a dress rehearsal.

Despite the poor response to our earlier concert with The Galliards we now had a regular audience at the Brighton Ballads and Blues club to draw on and had no hesitation in taking on the project and so it was that on 15 November 1961 we presented Pete Seeger in a one man concert at The Ralli Hall, Hove.

Admission was relatively expensive at 5/6 (27.5p) nevertheless it proved to be not only a sell out event but also a dynamic and memorable evening. To help offset the cost we managed to negotiate a television appearance in Southampton which was pre-recorded in the afternoon of the 15 November and transmitted immediately after the early evening news. Pete duly arrived in Hove but with a huge bough from a tree strapped to the roof of his car. At his request it took five bemused "volunteers" to carry the limb into the hall. Nobody asked how he got it on to the car to begin with but he did explain he had 'found it' lying beside the road. Its role only became apparent during the concert when he took a woodsman's axe out of a case and promptly chopped the bough in half while singing a lumberjack's work song.

BRIGHTON BALLADS & BLUES CLUB

present an evening with

PETE SEEGER.

The Great American Folk Singer

at

THE RALLI HALL, HOVE

OPPOSITE HOVE RAILWAY STATION

on

WEDNESDAY, 15 NOV.

at 7.30 p.m.

Admission 5/6

TICKETS AT THE DOOR or in advance from: C. Bennett
112 North Lane, East Preston, Sussex; also Club Members

Southern Folk Music Society Poster – Pete Seeger Concert – 1961. *The author*

The following day, 16 November 1961, under the headline "The joker and the jail threat" the Evening Argus ran the following story

"A rangy 42 year old American with the threat of a prison sentence hanging over him held a Hove audience spellbound for 2¹/₂hours last night. His name is Pete Seeger. His profession – folk singer.

And his crime-for which he was brought before the un-American activities Committee – is that he insists on singing the songs he likes and telling the jokes he likes. Some of them are of unions, the lot of the working man.

And when Seeger came before the committee, the same one which accused
playwright Arthur Miller, he was judged in contempt of Congress and was
sentenced to a year's imprisonment. The sentence was suspended.
Over here on bail, he returns to the United States next Tuesday and will go
before an appeals committee.

Forgotten . . .

But last night-when he took the stage of the Ralli Hall little more than an
hour after appearing before millions on television – his troubles were
forgotten as he entertained an audience of more than 200.
He launched himself into a programme of song and music with the versatility
and virtuosity that have made him the doyen of folk singers on both sides of
the Atlantic.
This almost seedy looking, 20th century troubadour with the gentle voice and
fantastic skill with string instruments sang numbers culled from a lifetime of
musical exploration, ranging through the earthy Negro blues, Scots sea
shanties and Irish melodies to a plaintive lament of the post-Hiroshima
Japanese.

Funny . . .

After a multi-encore ovation, Seeger spoke backstage of the ordeal he must
face in America.
"Sure the threat of prison hangs over me" he said "But I don't feel bitter. In
fact it's kinda funny if it wasn't so sad. I mean this sort of thing can hit some
people really hard.
They can lose their jobs for a start. But me . . . there's nowhere I can get
fired from."
His grin faded as he added "Of course, these terror tactics are quite wrong."
Seeger's appearance in Hove was organised by the Brighton Ballads and
Blues Club. It was his only appearance in the South of England, apart from
that tonight at the Albert Hall, London, where he is expected to perform
before an audience of 5,000 – RT"

I remember Pete had enormous charisma that few could match. On stage
he sang a chorus, held his hand in the air and called out "sing" and without
hesitation everybody did, almost as though it was being drawn out by some
magnetic force.

Meanwhile the club continued to flourish attracting people not only from
local towns but also several who 'hitch hiked' down each week from London.
Membership topped 350 and Long John Baldry made a return visit as guest
while the outstanding jazz guitarist Diz Disley 'dropped in' for a floor spot.
At Christmas however we received a demand for a substantial increase in rent
from £2.10.00 [£2.50] to £5 per week. Since that meant an audience of 40
people just to cover the cost of the room we were forced to seek new
accommodation and the final session at The Hideout was on 31 December.

On Sunday 7 January 1962, still in the afternoons, the club reopened in the Grill Room of Melbray's Restaurant, Kings Street [later to become the original Kings Club and now lost under The Brighton Thistle Hotel] with the late Alex Campbell making the first of many guest visits to Brighton. One slight problem was that the restaurant was open for lunchtime trade and the club had to adjust its starting time to 3.30pm instead of 3.00pm although still closing at 6.00pm. Nevertheless it appeared to make little difference to the support; membership continued to increase and people regularly travelled from as far afield as Bognor Regis and Crawley to attend the club. Over the next three months, guests at the new venue included Leon Rosselson, a return visit by Gerry Loughran, Hilda Syms, Wizz Jones, Louis Killen, folk journalist Eric Winter and – to complete the club's first six months – Rory McEwen [then the best known 'folk' singer in Britain through his regular TV appearances] who brought Bob Davenport with him. By then the club had enrolled over 500 members.

Brighton Ballads and Blues Club residents Sunday 8 October 1961. *left to right:* **Dick Richardson, Shirley Rose, the author, Geoff Rose and Terry Scarlett.** *The author*

Within the club the residents had changed. Geoff and Shirley Rose had 'retired' from the folk scene and Terry and I had been joined by 'Whispering' Bob McDonald of Brighton on mandolin, Valerie Greenfield of Worthing, vocals and Dick Richardson of Redhill, guitar and vocals. Terry, Valerie, Bob and myself, apart from singing as soloists also formed a group called "The Beachcombers" which then sub divided by various permutations into trios and duos.

Although similar clubs were opening throughout the country, Brighton was now well established nationally as a major folk song centre and Eric Winter in his weekly column in the Melody Maker referred to the club as the only one in the country with a view of the sea.

With the summer season approaching Melbray's Restaurant opened all day for Sunday trade and the club closed on 25 March with a commitment to its members to re-open in the autumn. The closure of this popular club was covered by the Brighton and Hove Gazette, which published the following story on Friday 16 March 1962:

"Making (folk) music

Sunday afternoons for hundreds of (mostly) young people in Sussex this winter have not meant watching ancient movies on television, but getting together to make music at the Brighton Ballads and Blues Club.

The club, an offshoot of the Southern Folk Music Society, began in September. Last Sunday the 500th member was enrolled. The occasion? A visit from one of Britain's leading folk singers, Rory McEwen.

Three people from the west (of Sussex) founded the club and play prominent parts in it's activities. President Terry Scarlett leads the club ensemble, which includes club chairman Clive Bennett, and secretary Betty Scarlett (Terry's wife), who collects the money at the door.

* * * * *

Despite it's popular success, the club, like many other winter lodgers in seaside resorts, will soon have outstayed it's welcome at it's seafront restaurant headquarters. After this month, Monday evening sessions will be held in Worthing instead.

Oddly enough, although a liking for folk music tends to be a sign of revolt against mass entertainment media, the regular folk spot on TV's "Tonight" programme has probably done more than any other factor to make the music more widely known and "respectable."

And Rory McEwen, with brother Alex, was the first of "Tonight's" folk singers. A tall, slim, dark suited man with a neckerchief and the air of a dandy on Sunday, he sang, to his own guitar accompaniment, *bothy ballads and blues with equal facility.

Folk people are nothing if not guitar fanatics, and Rory's big 12-stringed instrument, like the one **Leadbelly used to play, was the centre of attraction.

Instead of brother Alex, who was detained in Scotland, Rory brought Bob Davenport down from London.

Reputed to be able to make himself heard above the uproar of a Camden Town Irish pub, Bob sang, unaccompanied, Irish and Geordie songs about the I.R.A., about mining disasters, about wakes.

And when the club session was over, a hard core moved over to the back bar of the Wheatsheaf to make music in a more beery surrounding. Folk singing is thirsty-making work. – J.F.P.

* Bothies were huts used by Scottish farm labourers in the last century. Bothy ballads are the songs they made up.

** Nickname of Hudson Leadbetter, generally acknowledged as the greatest of all American folk singers."

When we announced the closure of the club for a summer break Terry and I were approached by a number of regulars with a request to run a club in Worthing. Since almost half of the 500 or more membership lived in or around that town we agreed to open a Ballads and Blues Club there for the

26

summer of 1962.

Back in Brighton however other regulars were concerned at losing their 'club' and this led to the creation of *'The Southern Folk Forum'*, Brighton's second folk club. A non-singer, Annie Tribe, was the instigator and she acted as Secretary with popular local duo Pat Howell and Bernie Cottam as residents and 'Whispering' Bob McDonald handling some of the publicity.

Scheduled to open on Thursday 19 April the date was changed to Tuesday 17 when it was realised the original date clashed both with the annual CND march from Aldermaston and a Count Basie concert at The Dome.

The delay in opening in 1962 was covered in The Evening Argus on Tuesday 27 March when it ran the following story:

" 'COUNT' DOWN FOR FOLK SONG

Basie and the Bomb put the clock back two days

The Campaign for Nuclear Disarmament and the Count Basie band. These two apparently unconnected combos have forced a new Brighton folk-singing club to change its opening night.

The Southern Folk Forum was to have sung its first song on April 19, the day before Good Friday.

Then the organisers discovered that most of its potential members would be preparing for the Easter Aldermaston march, and would not be able to attend the Forum.

"Those who aren't marching all seem to have planned to go to the Count Basie concert in Brighton on the same night," explained BOB McDONALD, mandolinist and guitarist, who is a founder member of the Forum.

Having decided that folk music was hardly bigger than both the C.N.D. and Count Basie, the fans stepped down, and chose another opening date.

The new Forum takes over where the Brighton Ballad and Blues Club left off, Bob told me. The B. and B. club has left Brighton for the summer and will form its headquarters in Worthing, where nearly half the members live.

"There was quite an outcry from Brightonians when they heard they were losing their club," said Bob, "so the Forum has been formed to fill the gap."

Its first night will be held at the City of London Arms, London Street, Brighton. Guest star will be ALEX CAMPBELL.

The date? Tuesday, April 17.

"That should satisfy everyone" said Bob, "including ban-the bomb marchers and Basie fans!"

Guest for the opening night was Alex Campbell and among the floor singers who 'dropped in' was Steve Benbow. A few weeks later when Steve appeared as guest he arrived with some friends for support including Hilda Syms, Russell Quaye and 'The City Ramblers'.

The club ran from 17 April to 26 August 1962 on Tuesday evenings at The City of London Arms, London Street [a pub which, like many others, no longer exists having been swallowed up in redevelopment]. Annie then decided to transfer the sessions to Friday evenings at The Volunteer in New Road. Unfortunately the landlord, confronted with what he considered to be a group of 'beatniks', arriving for the opening night session refused them entry and the club failed to open. Instead, under the guidance of Pat Howell and Bernie Cottam, it evolved during the early autumn into an informal singaround in The Wheatsheaf, Bond Street.

'Whispering' Bob McDonald.   **Bernie Cottam and Pat Howell.**
The author   *Tim Kent*

28

2 DEVELOPMENT IN BRIGHTON

THE LONG RUNNING CLUBS

In the autumn, on 7 October 1962, featuring Hilda Syms and Russell Quaye as guests, I re-opened the *'Brighton Ballads and Blues Club'* with Bob McDonald, Valerie Greenfield, Dick Richardson and Clare Clayton, a traditional singer from Hassocks, as co residents. Meetings were still held on Sunday afternoons but now on the second floor of Fullers Restaurant, 14 East Street, Brighton and here, on 14 October, Martin Carthy made his first appearance in Brighton.

The Southern Folk Music Society

PRESENTS

FOLK

at the Brighton Ballads & Blues Club

FULLER'S RESTAURANT

East Street :: Brighton

(SECOND FLOOR)

Every SUNDAY 3.30 to 6.30 p.m.

★ REGULAR APPEARANCE OF LONDON ARTISTES ★

Membership 1/-   Admission 2/6

Enquiries: C. BENNETT :: 112 NORTH LANE :: ANGMERING-ON-SEA :: SUSSEX

Southern Folk Music Society poster 1962. *The author*

Here again the club couldn't start until 3.30pm when the lunch time trade was over but we were able to continue until 6.30. The club was forced to close at these premises however on 16 December 1962 when Fullers decided there was not enough afternoon trade to make it economic staying open. It was then becoming increasingly difficult to find a suitable coffee bar or restaurant that remained open on a Sunday afternoon in mid-winter nevertheless, after much searching, the following week the club moved to the cellar of The Lorelei Coffee Bar [now the "Casa Don Carlos"] in The Lanes, with Louis Killen as the opening guest.

Southern Folk Music Society poster 1962/3. *The author*

Audiences for an afternoon coffee bar session had seriously declined which was reflected in the size of the new venue. Then, with the advent of summer and the

The Southern Folk Music Society presents

FOLK

AT THE

CELLAR

The Brighton Ballads & Blues Club

LORELEI COFFEE BAR

The Lanes :: Brighton

Every SUNDAY 3.30 to 6.30 p.m.

★ REGULAR APPEARANCE OF LONDON ARTISTES ★

Membership 1/6   Admission 3/-

Enquiries: C. BENNETT :: 112 NORTH LANE :: ANGMERING-ON-SEA :: SUSSEX various counter attractions offered in a seaside resort, the era of the coffee bar club was over and the sessions finally closed on 23 June 1963. Although it survived for only twenty months the Ballads and Blues club was by then known nationally and established Brighton as a corner stone of the revival.

Much earlier however, on 17 December 1961, whilst the club was still meeting in the Hideout Ballroom, a number of performers and friends, reluctant to stop singing at 6.00 pm when the afternoon session ended, adjourned to The Wheatsheaf, Bond Street. Like many others this pub no longer exists, although the building still stands and the name is embossed high up in the wall. There they settled down for a drink and informal singaround in the back bar. This soon became the normal pattern following on from the afternoon sessions but when the club closed for the summer they also stopped. When the club re-opened in the autumn of 1962 they resumed and by late November had become a regular 'informal' session, lasting for much of the evening. With the retirement of 'Nellie' the well-known landlady, the sessions eventually transferred to the Running Horse in King Street - another pub that was soon to succumb to the developers.

On 3 March 1963 this informal session transferred to The Heart In Hand, North Road and under the guidance of Johnie Winch soon became the *'Country and Gospel Club'* – **Brighton's third folk club**. By now Rod Machling had emerged as a fine singer/guitarist and shared the residency with Johnie. The club was soon so popular and the room so small that in the autumn of 1963 it became necessary to find larger premises and the club moved to The Stanford Arms, Preston Circus.

The folk 'boom' was now well underway and every Sunday evening the clubroom filled with people. There was still a strong American influence on the material performed; Negro blues and gospel songs mixed easily with traditional numbers from America, Ireland, Scotland and England. Virtually all performers used a guitar for simple accompaniment and songs with an easy chorus, allowing everyone to join in, were the most popular. The acclaimed master of gospel songs was Johnie, sometimes called 'Reverend' Johnie, Winch.

At the same time Johnie and Rod expanded their club organising by opening the first Eastbourne Folk Club, also on Sunday evenings. To cover these double appearances each took turns alternating between Brighton and Eastbourne. One week Johnny was in Brighton with Rod in Eastbourne and the next week it was the other way round.

In January 1965 the Stanford sessions were renamed *'Brighton Singers Club'*, still organised by Johnie and Rod but in the name of Southern Folk Enterprises.

Johnie and Rod remained the residents plus, from time to time, various other singers including Brian Golbey, Phil Sears and Mick Johnson. As Jim Marshall recalls it was during this time that Tom Paxton made a couple of visits to the club, first as a last minute replacement for Alex Campbell and later, in February 1966, as a guest in his own right. Rod, incidentally, played a guitar he made for himself and two years later made a second one which he played regularly until dropping out of the folk circuit.

Johnie Winch. *Jim Marshall*

Rod Machling. *Jim Marshall*

Brighton Country & Gospel Club poster 1963. *Jim Marshall*

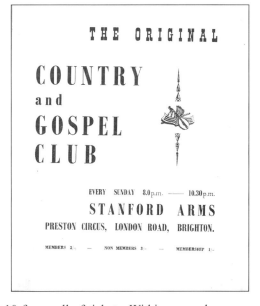

There was a short break from April to June 1966 when the club closed but on 12 June 1966 it reopened as *'The Stanford Folk Club'* with Rod Machling and Brian Golbey from Ditchling as residents while Jim Marshall and Dennis Baverstock took care of the organising. There was a 'Come-All-Ye' for opening night and with admission at 2/6 [12¹/₂p] the total receipts were £3.2.6 against which Jim had expenditure of £1.12.10 for a roll of tickets. Within a year however admission had been amended to 3/6 [17¹/₂p] for members and 4/6 [22¹/₂p] non members and membership was set at 2/= [10p]. In 1966 incidentally the club opened on Christmas Day – Sunday 25th December. Three years after re-opening, on 13 June 1969, Jim Marshall, writing in the Brighton and Hove Gazette, reflected on the early years by saying *"Three years ago this Sunday*

the present Stanford Arms Folk Club came into being. On that first night there was an audience of 25 and a grand total of two singers, Brian Golbey and Rod Machling. The club survived those early, very shaky, days and is now one of the best established clubs in the country, if the views of visiting singers are anything to go by."

SOUTHERN FOLK ENTERPRISES

===== presents =====

The

BRIGHTON SINGERS CLUB

Introducing every week
acclaimed artists from
- England and America -

at

THE STANFORD ARMS
Preston Circus, London Road
BRIGHTON

: **Every Sunday Night** :

from 8 to 10.30 p.m.

ADMISSION	OPENING	ANNUAL MEMBERSHIP
2/6d.	17 JAN	2/6d.

COME TO
BRIGHTON'S SUNDAY FOLK MUSIC CLUB
SPRINGFIELD HOTEL
Springfield Road

EVERY SUNDAY at 8pm

Students, Holidaymakers and Singers Always Welcome

Brighton Singers Club poster 1965.
Jim Marshall
[above right] **Brian Golbey.**
Jim Marshall
Brighton Sunday Folk Club poster
1976 *Jim Marshall*

The club remained at The Stanford Arms until 21 December 1975 by which time Jim Marshall had become the sole organiser. On 28 December 1975 as *'Brighton's Sunday Club'* it transferred to The Springfield, Springfield Road where it remained until closing on 30 September 1984.

A month later on 28 October 1984, still on a Sunday evening, it rose like a phoenix as 'Berties Folk Night' meeting at The Prince Albert, Trafalgar Street and continued there under the guidance of Jim Marshall until 1 February 1987.

To date this has been the longest running folk session in Brighton with roots reaching back almost 26 years and during all this time has maintained the earlier clubs policy of bringing the finest national and international performers of the day from a wide range of folk styles to Brighton.

The list of guests is phenomenal and includes such diverse performers as the legendary blind Negro blues singer Reverend Gary Davis, zany humorist Jasper Carrott, the Virginian bluegrass guitarist Bill Clifton, controversial Irish poet, writer and singer Dominic Behan, exciting Latin American exponents Dorita y Pepe, one man band Don Partridge both before and after achieving acclaim with his hit song 'Rosie', famed American singer Derroll Adams, first lady of British blues Jo-Ann Kelly, Davy Graham, John Renbourn, Ralph McTell, Dick Gaughan, Shetland fiddle player Aly Bain, the American Arlo Guthrie – son of Woodie, Hedy West, brilliant jazz guitarist and entertainer Diz Disley, Stefan Grossman, Tom Paley, Mike Seeger, Peggy Seeger, renowned traditional performers The Copper Family, George Spicer, Martin Carthy, Dave Swarbrick, contemporary songwriter Leon Rosselson, the pride of Sussex – Shirley Collins, Boys of The Lough, Robin Hall and Jimmie MacGregor, Isabel Sutherland, Tim Hart, Maddy Prior and, for many the father figure of the British folk revival, Ewan MacColl. Add to this virtually every other significant singer in the country and you start to appreciate how the club maintained a tremendous reputation for such a long period.

That reputation however also included the standards set by a highly impressive list of residents. As mentioned above, it started with Johnie and Rod and then Rod and Brian Golbey. Brian turned professional in January 1967 and left the area the following year when he teamed up with Pete

Stanley and with their brand of American Old Timey and bluegrass songs formed one of the most talented and popular duos produced in the folk clubs.

Miles Wootton
and Allan Taylor
at BBC Radio Brighton.
Jim Marshall

33

The club then adopted a policy of having different residents for monthly periods partnering Rod. These included Allan 'Spud' Taylor, Eddie Upton, Paul Setford, Miles Wootton, Jerry Jordan, Derek Lockwood and the precocious Tim Broadbent who started singing in folk clubs at the age of 14 when, as Vic Smith wrote in the Mid Sussex Times on 10 May 1979, *"... he had a prodigious guitar technique, a fine singing voice and a confidence in his performance that belied his years."*

Rod left to get married in October 1967 and soon after this the highly acclaimed singing/songwriting team of Miles Wootton and Allan 'Spud' Taylor took over as residents. 'Spud' turned professional in December 1969 and moved away to Leeds and his place was taken by Tim Broadbent.

In July 1971 Marie Curtis joined the team of residents but left in January 1972 to marry fellow singer Alan White and move away to Birmingham, both of them having entered the 'professional' singers ranks. Two singers, Pam Fereday and Ivor Pickard, working on an alternate week basis, then took her place until Ivor left during 1974.

Tim Broadbent *and* **Marie Curtis.**
Jim Marshall

By 1976, when the club transferred to The Springfield, the residents were Miles, Tim and Pam but within a few months their ranks expanded with the arrival of John Collyer. Tim took a break in 1978 returning on an occasional basis the following year before finally leaving in 1983. Later additions to the residents were Pete Cartlidge [1978], Christine Hase, Don and Fiona Watts [1980], Kevin Barber, John Bickford, Malcom and Julia Donaldson [1982], Stuart Reed. Alan White – who had moved back to the town from Birmingham – and Marilyn Bennett [1983]. Malcolm Donaldson was a doctor at the Royal Sussex Hospital and Julia a teacher in Brighton. In addition she was a prolific song writer and apart from the many funny and well constructed songs they performed in folk clubs she also wrote songs for 'Playschool' and 'Playaway' on BBC television and wrote and performed in the show 'King Grunt's Cake' at the Gardner Centre in 1977.

Ivor Pickard *[left]and*
Pam Fereday *[above]. Jim Marshall*

When the club subsequently moved to the Prince Albert the residents were Kevin Barber, Marilyn Bennett, Barry Walker, Ron Brecher, Alan Murray and Eddie Upton. This was also the point when Miles Wootton left the line up after over seventeen years as a resident at the Sunday club in its various guises.

John Bickford and Kevin Barber.
Jim Marshall

Malcolm and Julia Donaldson.
Challis Bousfield

35

John Collyer and Tim Broadbent.
Jim Marshall

Ron Brecher and Alan Murray.
Jim Marshall

The changes of venue led to no reduction in the standard of guests and those featured included, on 29 June 1980 Jean Ritchie, one of the most respected of all American traditional singers and during 1982 The Watersons, Ossian, Richard Digance, the brilliant multi talented American Peter Rowan and the Oyster Band.

Barry Walker & Marilyn Bennett.
Jim Marshall

The standard of the early residents is clear when you see how their careers developed. Johnie Winch turned professional moving first to Hastings and then Germany in 1973 from where he toured extensively in Europe before returning to live in Hastings until the end of the century when he again moved abroad to live once again in Germany. When Allan Taylor joined the professional ranks he signed a five-year recording contract with Liberty – United Artists soon after a much-praised concert tour with Fairport Convention. Brian Golbey, who had been associated with the Brighton Country Music Club at The Springfield in 1964 prior to becoming a resident at the Sunday folk club, also turned professional after about a year and then moved to London from where, as already mentioned, he toured first in a highly successful country music partnership with Pete Stanley and then as a soloist, during which time he appeared in Nashville and met and played with some of the top country singers in the

36

USA. Tim Broadbent launched himself into a professional career as a singer at the age of nineteen. Like many other singers he soon found regular work on the continent and made Germany his base for a few years where he teamed up with Johnie Winch. Ivor Pickard was another who embarked on a professional career abroad, based in Germany, before returning to Sussex to live in Hastings.

Alan White. *John Collyer*

During their singing partnership at The Stanford Allan Taylor and Miles Wootton also enjoyed a highly rated career as song writers. In 1975 Allan Taylor and Brian Golbey united to form two-thirds of the group 'Cajun Moon'. Since both these outstanding musicians had been residents at the same club a decade earlier this partnership was possibly inevitable, the only surprise being it took so long to occur.

Alan White, like many other popular performers in the local folk clubs, was not a native. He arrived in the town to read for a degree at Brighton Polytechnic and whilst there started making a name for himself as a singer and writer of comic songs. After completing his degree he decided to go fully professional giving his reason, as Vic Smith reported in the Mid Sussex Times on 19 February 1976, *"To prove to myself that I can do it and get it out of my system.".* He eventually moved away to Birmingham but returned after two years, settling to what he originally wanted to do, which was teach.

Although the Sunday's club founder Johnie Winch moved on after only three years, continuity was provided by Jim Marshall, who was a club regular during those first formative years, before becoming organiser and going on to run the club for the next 21 years. One of the few on the folk club scene who was a 'non singer', Jim operated as 'mine host' from the rear of the clubroom rather than 'up front'. From this position he not only gathered the admission fees but was also the critically important initial contact for people attending a folk club for the first time.

As we shall see later it was not just the Sunday folk club that was to benefit from Jim's contacts with people both oral and written as he became a key element in the local media, first through the Brighton and Hove Gazette and then via BBC Local Radio.

The eventual closure of this, the area's second longest running folk club, in February 1987 after 24 years [26 if you accept an informal linkage to the original Ballads and Blues club], did not however deter Jim Marshall for long and on 10 April 1987 he opened a new club, generally monthly on a Friday evening, again at The Stanford Arms, Preston Circus. They continued at this venue until 29 October 1990 and then on 7 December transferred to the Springfield Hotel - history repeating itself. A year later on 5 December 1991 the sessions became regular fortnightly meetings on Thursdays but in June 1992 the brewery sold the pub and with an uncertain future the club closed on 18 June for a 'summer break'. The 'summer' proved to be a long one and not until 15 April 1993 did its successor reopen at The Royal Oak, Station Street, Lewes.

[left] **Jim Marshall collecting entrance fees** – *in this case from John Towner, member of The Mariners and one of the organisers of the Black Horse Folk Club at Telham near Hastings.*
[right] **Allan Taylor and Brian Golbey.** *Both Jim Marshall*

Meantime back in April 1963 at the Ballads and Blues Club in The Lorelei, Dick Richardson left the residents and teamed up with Mike Rogers from Crawley to run, for a few brief weeks from 14 April until 19 May, **Brighton's fourth folk club**, meeting on Sunday afternoons in The Aquarium.

This was followed on 7 June 1963 by the opening of **Brighton's fifth folk club** at the Teachers Training College Students Hostel and Social Club in Marine Parade with 'Whispering' Bob McDonald and myself as first night guests.

In the autumn of 1963, with a regular Sunday session now organised in Brighton by Johnie Winch, I decided that rather than seeking to re-open the Brighton Ballads and Blues club, I would opt instead for an out of town session. This led to the founding of the first Shoreham Folk Song Club meeting weekly on Tuesday evenings. Bob McDonald, Valerie Greenfield and myself were again the residents and after several appearances as a floor singer we invited Jack Whyte, a Scot recently arrived in Brighton, to join us – which he did during January 1964. Shortly afterwards he was to become another major influence in the development of the local folk scene.

Terry Masterson and Jack Whyte.
Terry Masterson

By then Paul Setford from Worthing had also become a regular floor singer at the Shoreham club. Like Jack he was later to become a key figure in the area when he succeeded Jack as organiser and resident of one of Brighton's longest running folk clubs.

During February Jack Whyte enlisted the assistance of Terry Masterson, then based in London, and on 6 March 1964, they opened *'Friday's Folk'* – Brighton's **sixth folk song club**, meeting every Friday in the club room of The Springfield Hotel, Springfield Road. The first floor singer on that opening night was Paul Setford.

Although Terry had agreed to join Jack in his Brighton venture he was unable to be there on the opening night due to a commitment teaching guitar at a Richmond evening institute. He eventually arrived on 27 March and acted as co-host for the next three years until 13 July 1967 when Jack and his wife Helena departed for Canada.

This club continued to meet at the Springfield until March 1981 when it transferred briefly – until July 1982 – to The Stanford Arms, Preston Circus before returning to The Springfield on 6 August 1982 where it finally closed on 8 March 1985 on its twenty first anniversary.

Organised initially by Jack, he was succeeded in August 1967 by Terry then, when Terry decided to concentrate on running his other club in Lewes, by Paul Setford and Laurie Goddard assisted, for a while, by Audrey Judd.

When Paul 'retired' after almost eleven years, from September 1969 until July 1980, Eddie Upton took over and was later joined by George Wagstaff. Finally this duo gave way to Val Wagstaff. This is to-date the area's third longest running club.

Mention was made earlier of the numerous 'Residents' from the Sunday club who went on to make a career, albeit for some only briefly, from singing. Of those involved with Friday's Folk the most notable professional was Eddie Upton who went on to earn his living, from both folk song and dance. Initially, in his spare time, he was both singing and calling with the Etchingham Steam Band when he decided to leave his job at the bank and become a mature student at Sussex University reading politics. Whilst at University he became involved with the Albion Band as caller and after obtaining his degree took up a post as Folk Artiste in Residence in Gateshead with the Libraries and Arts Department, the first such post in the country. This was for twelve months but was subsequently extended for a further two years. He then moved to Somerset where he was instrumental in setting up and then becoming Director of Folk South West, an organisation devoted to promoting the performing arts.

Eddie Upton *[left]* **and Paul Setford** *[below]*.
Both Jim Marshall

Although all types of folk song and music were included at Friday's Folk the emphasis was on traditional material and early guests included A L 'Bert' Lloyd, Cyril Tawney, Robin Hall and Jimmie MacGregor, Christy Moore, Nic Jones, John Kirkpatrick, Harry Boardman, Bob Davenport, Frankie Armstrong, Alistair Anderson, Isabel Sutherland, Packie Byrne, Roy Harris, Martyn Wyndham-Read, Fred Jordan and the ubiquitous Alex Campbell. Perhaps the biggest 'snip' was 10 January 1969 when Terry managed to book Paco Pena for his one and only club booking for the princely sum of £30. Which was twice the amount Terry had originally offered.

This club was also responsible, at Terry's instigation, for the introduction of regular 'Special Traditional Evenings' devoted to local traditional singers. His motivation, as he recalls, was to introduce source singers to the younger generation frequenting folk clubs.

The first of these 'Specials', advertised for 22 September 1967, was a celebration of the eighty-first birthday of Sussex concertina player Scan Tester. Apart from Scan who was accompanied by his daughter Daisy, the guests that night were Cyril Phillips, Clare Clayton and George Belton. Initial reaction was a little mixed because at the end of the evening, in conversation with a newcomer to the club, the response he received was that it had been a good evening but "what were all those 'old boys' doing there?" Leaving Terry to explain that as source singers they were of prime importance providing the link between the folk revival and the tradition.

Another significant innovation created by Terry was the introduction of 'theme' evenings instead of guest nights. Local singers were encouraged to perform songs based on a pre-advertised theme and possibly to dress appropriately. These proved a great success and also became a regular feature of the club.

Scan Tester's 81st birthday celebration in Friday's Folk, Springfield Arms 22 Sept 1967. *[right]* **George Belton** *[standing] and* **Scan Tester** *[seated].* *[below]* **Cyril Phillips.** *Both photos by Tom Groome Reproduced courtesy of Ron Pope*

Like the Sunday club this long running session not only continued to bring top national and international performers to the town but also enjoyed, over the years, a string of outstanding residents. Unlike the Sunday club however there were numerous changes of organiser and a non-performing doorman, Laurie Goddard, provided continuity.

Laurie, like Jim Marshall at the Stanford, was content to sit

41

just outside the club room where he could hear the songs but still talk to people about local folk activities whilst collecting their admission money. Gregarious and friendly Laurie was, again like Jim Marshall, an immensely important part of the folk club. Serving Friday's Folk through its entire life of 21 years he was not only known to all the singers and regulars but was an incalculable benefit to the local scene as the first contact for many newcomers to folk music.

Friday's Folk Club
Programme 1967/8. *The author*

Laurie Goddard. *Jim Marshall*

During the mid 1970's the folk boom was at its height not just in Britain but right across Europe. The result was that during the summer months when foreign students poured into the area in their thousands to attend the many English language schools in the vicinity one of their priorities was to go to a folk club, usually accompanied by the group leader. Financially they were a great advantage to the club organiser since it was not uncommon for two separate groups of twenty or more students

to turn up for the evening and the club's income increased dramatically allowing it to bank something for the winter months when attendances returned to normal. For the club regulars however they were not always quite so welcome since they were sometimes noisy and the crowded clubroom could become just too hot for comfort.

Jim Marshall remembers visiting Friday's Folk at the Springfield one week and standing, as he often did, outside the clubroom talking to Laurie Goddard whilst listening to the singing from inside. Within the club there was a slightly lower than average size crowd and all was relatively quiet and low key. He glanced out of the window and saw a line of twenty-five to thirty students, although at first glance it looked many more, snaking its way across the road towards the pub. There was clearly only one place so many people were going at the same time and it transformed the evening at a stroke. This type of experience was typical of all the Brighton and Eastbourne clubs although rather less so in Lewes.

One response was for the clubs to open for a second evening each week during the 'student' season. Ostensibly it would be for the foreign visitors but locals were also welcome. In 1978 the three resident singers from the Springfield Sunday club formed themselves into an occasional trio called 'Patchwork' presenting a Tuesday evening folk session at the pub for students.

[above] **Roger Brasier.**
Tom Groome [courtesy Ron Pope]

[above left] **Dave Jenkin, Barry Walker and Marilyn Bennett**
Jim Marshall

[left] **Ivor George.**
George Wagstaff

Charlotte Oliver & Richard Spong.
George Wagstaff

Val Wagstaff.
George Wagstaff

[left] **Sandra Goddard at Friday's Folk with John Ticehurst** *[seated].*
George Wagstaff

To return to the residents, apart from the organisers Jack and Terry then Paul Setford and Eddie Upton there were a number of excellent performers who served at various times as residents. One of the first was Keith Johns followed by Don and Sarah Morgan, Will Duke, Tony Walsh, Maria Loughran, Sandra Goddard, Roger Brasier, Barry Ruffell, Dave Jenkin, Jerry Jordan, Mavis Sawdy, Charlotte Oliver, Charlie Watts, Ivor George and John Ticehurst – who had a heart attack and died in the club room during a meeting on 21 January 1983, shortly after he had sung. The guest singer on that traumatic evening was John Kirkpatrick.

Of all the talented floor singers that have graced the local folk clubs over the past 37 years John Ticehurst perhaps deserves special mention. A modest and rather shy man he, together with two friends Ron Pope and Tom Groome all of whom lived in Eastbourne and had been involved in running the first

Eastbourne Folk Club, were regular visitors to clubs in Brighton, Eastbourne and Lewes. When the Merrie England club opened in Eastbourne in 1972 they were among the first there and virtually every week were the first to arrive to claim their usual seats in the second row. It was soon obvious to the organisers by the way John joined in the choruses of songs that he not only could sing but also knew all the words of many of the songs. After several months of gentle persuasion from the club's residents and encouragement from his two friends he finally took the stage for his début as a floor singer.

He was an immediate success, a natural singer with a penchant for Sussex songs, particularly those of the Copper family. It was not long before he became a regular performer at The Springfield, Brighton, Lewes Arms, Lewes and The Crown, Eastbourne on Friday, Saturday and Sunday evenings each week, culminating in becoming a resident at Friday's Folk Club.

His sudden and untimely death at the relatively early age of 58 was felt across the county and his funeral was attended by a host of folk enthusiasts. Three weeks later George Wagstaff accompanied by a number of John's friends including Val Wagstaff, Ron Pope, Roger Watson and Sandra Goddard scattered his ashes on 'Copper country', the Downs above Rottingdean which had been so close to his heart and where in 1924 the ashes of James 'Brasser' Copper had been returned to the soil.

Sandra Goddard recalls that John had told her his father used to sing in a pub at Polegate and had a repertoire that included many variants of songs usually associated with the Coppers.

John Ticehurst.
Tom Groome [courtesy Ron Pope]

Keith Johns.
Jim Marshall

Reflecting on untimely deaths, another loss to the folk scene was Keith Johns who died at the age of 50 on 17 January 1994 after some twelve years of suffering from Multiple Sclerosis.

Keith arrived in Brighton around 1966 from Rochester, Kent. It was there, whilst at college, that he had encountered a flat-pick guitarist and got 'hooked' on the instrument. Then, after 'hanging around' with the chap for a few months, he worked out how it was done and set about singing and playing and became a highly skilled performer. Keith was a fine performer with both guitar and mandolin, particularly of country and blues material, and his cheeky grin and impudent humour made him immensely popular with his contemporaries. In addition he was also famed for the craftsmanship of his beautiful hand made guitars, one of which was owned by Ralph McTell.

Another Brighton based maker of fine instruments was John Roberts who produced superb mandolins and mountain dulcimers. His death in the early 1980's following an accident meant he was 'ss well known than his skills warranted but John Collyer, who has one of his dulcimers, describes it as "magnificent".

These long running clubs all have links with the first folk song club in The Hideout in East Street on a Sunday afternoon during the autumn of 1961. Since then many other folk song clubs, mostly without direct links to the original club – although many have had some contact with members of Brighton's early folk scene – have opened in the town, but only one survives today.

Friday's Folk Club organisers 1983:
Laurie Goddard, Val and George Wagstaff.
Jim Marshall

Before discussing them it would seem appropriate to digress slightly, for in parallel with the revival of interest in folk song there developed an interest in an American cousin – Country Music. The first local club for followers of this music form opened in 1964 as the *'Brighton Country and Western Club'*, meeting on Wednesday evenings at the Springfield Hotel. The club was founded by Eric Neville, David Lloyd, Jim Marshall – who became such a significant figure on the local folk scene – and the superb multi instrumentalist and singer Brian Golbey who soon after became resident at the Brighton Singers Club in the Stanford Arms. The aim, as with the folk clubs, was to bring the best of Country music to the town and early guests included the Strawberry Hill Boys, Talking John Berry and the Malcolm Price Trio.

Brighton Country Music Club organisers:
Eric Neville, Brian Golbey, David Lloyd and Jim Marshall.
Jim Marshall

Brighton Country Music Club poster 1964.
Jim Marshall

[below] **Neil Coppendale, Bill Monroe and Jim Marshall.** *Jim Marshall*

The venture proved popular but lasted only one year, going out with a 'bang' with Bill Clifton as the guest when the organisers recognised they were booking virtually the same performers as the local folk clubs. At about this time Jim Marshall and Brian Golbey also became involved with re-opening the Sunday night folk sessions at the Stanford Arms.

These country sessions were acoustic but the later and long running Country and Western club which had no links with the original 1964 club was much more commercial with full amplification. This was organised by Neil Coppendale and opened in 1971. Meeting at various venues, it started at The Richmond then, in 1978, moved to the Madeira Hotel, Marine Parade and later to the Concorde followed by the King Alfred in Hove and finally the Labour Club in Lewes Road.

One feature of all the early clubs was the total reliance on imported guest singers "Regular Appearance of London Artistes" as some notices advertised. As the folk 'boom' gathered pace many of these 'imported' semi professional guests either joined agencies or asked the club organiser to sign some form of contract. These were of course 'loaded' in favour of the singer with a clause that allowed a substitute of the singer's choice to be sent to the club if the named guest had to cancel while the club, if it wanted to cancel was still liable for the full fee. Many organisers initially thought, possibly rather naïvely, this guaranteed the appearance of their guest and in most cases it did, although there were inevitably occasional cancellations due to illness or travel problems when the weather was bad which were accepted by a club organiser. Sometimes however things went seriously wrong when the guest cancelled at the last minute or worse just did not arrive. Unfortunately this problem usually applied to the big named guest and club organisers soon learnt with much frustration and embarrassment that the so-called contract was virtually meaningless at these times. A good example was supplied by Jim Marshall when in the Brighton Folk Diary No.4 for July and August 1970 he inserted the following notice concerning the non-appearance of Louis Killen. As Jim recalls he never did receive a reply or any explanation and at the club on the 26 April at the end of the evening he spent some time refunding part of the admission to all the audience.

"Louis Killen – an explanation
We greatly regret that, despite the fact that we had a signed contract with WILLOW MANAGEMENT (owned by ROYSTON WOOD), LOUIS KILLEN did NOT appear as arranged on April 26th. The club received no prior notification that Louis Killen would not appear, nor was any reply received to our registered letter sent to Willow management enquiring why Mr. Killen did not turn up. The matter is now in the hands of a solicitor."

There was however a silver lining to the problem, both the numbers and standard of local singers performing floor spots increased rapidly and eventually clubs started using the more competent Sussex based singers as guests – still mixed with a programme of imported 'professional' guests from London and beyond. In addition, this development of local performers enabled clubs to introduce "Come All Ye" evenings specifically for the residents and floor singers and also encouraged the expansion of local clubs since there were so many singers available for floor spots and increasingly as low priced guests. Jim Marshall noted in the Brighton and Hove Gazette on 22 August 1975.

" . . . one rather nice thing about clubs in this area is the fact that they

regularly book local singers as guests rather than relying completely on the full time professionals. I suppose we're lucky in having so many excellent singers living locally."

This was not however the first time that the quality of local performers had been noted. Vic Smith, writing in the Brighton and Hove Herald on 22 May 1970, with only a hint of the outstanding talents of professionals such as Johnie Winch, Allan Taylor, Brian Golbey and Alan White, recorded:

"A lot of the guests who have been booked at local clubs have told me they have been either very stimulated or very frightened by the prospect of a Brighton appearance. The reason for both these states of mind seems to have been the very high standard of the residents and floor singers in the area.

Certainly, the standard is high. We have a number of fully professional singers in the town. Peter Collins and Roger Hubbard both have recording contracts, Terry Masterson, Miles Wootton and Tim Broadbent are all to be heard singing on radio and television. "

Vic Smith, again, writing in the 'Herald' on 27 February 1970 about the Springfield Folk Club reported:

"....The usual residents are joined by Jerry Jordan for this evening. Singers like Jerry are the backbone of a good folk club; he is not in it for the money, but merely for the love of the music, and he will always help out by giving a few songs. I think his rich resonant voice is heard to best effect on unaccompanied traditional ballads, surely the most difficult type of singing to do well. With tonight's theme we may well be hearing his excellent versions of "Young Edwin in the Lowlands" and "The Flying Cloud"."

Four club favourites.
[left to right]
Sarah Morgan, Don Morgan, Jerry Jordan and Bryan Blanchard.
Jim Marshall

While Jerry Jordan in many ways typified the local floor singer two sisters, Anne and Maria Loughran, reflected the friendly inter club relationship. Jerry was and is an ardent member of the folk fraternity. He started performing floor spots in the early 60's and is still a regular and popular artiste today almost 40 years later.

Anne Loughran was one of the resident singers at the Lewes Arms folk club in 1976 and at about the same time her sister Maria was to be heard performing as a resident at Friday's Folk in Brighton. Later they were joined by Jenn Price to form 'Little Edith's Treat' and were a popular trio at all the local clubs playing a wide range of instruments including harmonium, fiddle, concertina, banjo and recorder. They sang in harmony and had a repertoire covering traditional songs and dance tunes, temperance ballads and drawing room songs.

3 DEVELOPMENT IN BRIGHTON

THE LATER CLUBS

Two of the earliest of the later clubs enjoyed a 'special' status. Partly because they met only during the academic year from mid October through until May with breaks for Christmas and Easter. Partly because although they were open to anyone from the area they had a virtual captive audience making it unnecessary to advertise for external support. Finally and indeed to a large degree, because they had financial security from an annual subsidy as a students campus facility. Most ordinary folk clubs faced with a shortfall in income had to rely on the organiser meeting the deficit from his or her own pocket. The 'special' cases were, of course, the University and College of Education Folk Clubs.

Possibly the most difficult local club to trace is *The BCE (Brighton College of Education) folk club* which, as already mentioned, started as **Brighton's fifth folk club** in March 1963 as the Teachers Training College Folk Club. In 1966 on 8 April John Eccles, in a major article on four clubs at the heart of the local folk scene, wrote in the Brighton and Hove Herald

"Nearer Brighton's student colleges is the Richmond where regulars can hear beating feet and hoarse singing on a Tuesday evening. Run by students of the College of Education, the Richmond Folk Club is presented by 21-year-old John Boler, a member of CND and one of those responsible for the huge success of the Julie Felix/Alex Campbell concert at the Dome some weeks ago. In a larger room with a greater percentage of students in the audience, traditional folk music is taken far more seriously here than in other clubs."

By January 1970 it was running at Falmer and on a Friday evening and in November 1971 they advertised an appearance by Steeleye Span, but nothing then until the following year.

On 4 October 1972 the 'club' transferred to The Pier Hotel, Marine Parade where it was advertised on Wednesdays until February 1974 with major guests including Jasper Carrot, Mike Marran, Dave Burland, Robin Dransfield and Diz Disley.

The steady flow of information through the 1972/4 period may have had something to do with Paul Downes. Paul, originally from Exeter, had moved to Brighton to attend the college and had already attained a high standard as a musician on a variety of instruments, and during 1972-73 became a regular performer both at the college and local clubs. Later he teamed up with Phil Beer, also from Exeter, to form a talented and successful duo and left college to embark on a career as a full time folk performer.

**Paul Downes &
Phil Beer
at the Stanford folk
club.** *Jim Marshall*

By 1976 their bookings were so numerous and widespread that they moved base to Cheltenham as it was more convenient for the motorway network. Then, like many others, they found there was a large amount of work for folk musicians on the continent. Paul moved back to Brighton, before eventually going solo while Phil moved on, first to the Albion Band and then to team up with Steve Knightley to form the highly acclaimed Show of Hands. Paul's brother Warwick, who played double bass, was also based in the town during this period with a musical instrument shop in Upper North Street and from time to time joined the duo for bookings.

There was further mention of the BCE club by Jim Marshall from time to time in his weekly column in the Brighton and Hove Gazette but this was sporadic because the organisers didn't supply information on a regular basis.

Almost as difficult to identify is the *University of Sussex folk club*. Jim Marshall, in his weekly review in the Brighton and Hove Gazette, mentions the appearance of Louis Killen at the University folk club on 6 February 1968, which would suggest the club was open in the autumn of 1967 if not before. This is probably **Brighton's eighth folk club**. In October 1968 Johnny Handle appeared as a guest and Jim continued to mention the club through 1969, when it met on Tuesday evenings. Guests included the Yetties on 7 October 1969 and a month later in November Tim Hart and Maddy Prior. There was an advert in the Folk Diary for 3 March 1970 with meetings at Falmer House although subsequent advertisements were rare. That year it opened on a Monday but met thereafter on Tuesdays. In 1973 it changed to Thursdays, opening on 11 October and guests included Leon Rosselson. The guests for early 1974 were listed as A L 'Bert' Lloyd, Steve Tilson, Magic Lantern, Leon Rosselson, John and Sue Kirkpatrick, Nic Jones and Stan Arnold. A year later they included Pete and Chris Coe, Dave Burland, Robin and Barry Dransfield, Richard Digance, Peter Bellamy, Nic Jones and Roy Harris. The last published date in the Folk Diary for a meeting was 18 March 1975 although there was a club

Ceilidh in December 1975 and Vic Smith on 26 February 1976 in his weekly column for the Mid Sussex Times wrote

"After a couple of terms lying fallow, the University of Sussex folk club is back in action this term, and next Thursday they have a very attractive evening in store with John James."

Returning to John Eccles' article in April 1966 he went on to say

"The next club I visited turned out to be the most relaxed, friendly and communal. Thursday night's "Fennario" Folk at the Prince George Inn is a gay mixture of clinking glasses, audience singing and half-a-dozen lads of all shapes and professions, playing any handy instrument. Organised by Oxfam to which all profits go, the club is led by 21-year-old bank clerk Eddie Upton. Eddie told me proudly that since September last year, when the club got under way, £25 had been handed over to Oxfam. "It may not be much but we had a lot of fun raising it" Eddie told me. Celebrity singers like Diz Disley, Nancy Whiskey and Ian McCann gave their services free at the club. "We specialise in sea shanties but that's only because I can't play the guitar," added Eddie. One tangible result of the club's formation is a unique sea shanty group called the Halyards. Led by Eddie they sing without instruments in clubs all over Sussex."

The photograph accompanying the article shows a group of singers comprising Bill Evans, Jerry Jordan, Derek Lockwood, Eddie, Paul Holden and Tony Foulkes. Whilst these sessions had clearly started in September 1965 it is unclear how much longer the meetings survived. It was not long however before Derek, Eddie and Paul, who formed the Halyards, changed the groups name to The Juggs, which brings me to the first of the later clubs meeting in the town and open to the general public. This, **Brighton's seventh folk club**, was a monthly meeting at the City of London in London Street with the interesting name of *'The Bottle and Juggs Club'*, named after the resident group The Juggs. The group had by then achieved a reputation for superb harmonies and unaccompanied singing of traditional songs and sea-chanties but for some time prior to merging their talents schoolmaster Derek Lockwood, along with Eddie and Paul had each become established as a fine solo performer. Jim Marshall writing in the Brighton and Hove Gazette on 23 June 1967 noted that the club was *"Currently being held monthly"* and that *"On Thursday next, June 29, they have as their first guest singers, the Young Tradition"*. A week earlier he had reported that the club would be running weekly from September but on the 14 July he noted *"The recent non-appearance of the advertised guests at the City of London provided an excellent opportunity for the many local traditional singers there to show how extremely capable they are of providing an evening of very high standard entertainment"*. Unfortunately there is no further mention of the club and in that respect it could be argued that it barely lasted long enough to be recognised as a formal club.

Also in 1967 there was, all too briefly, a blues club organised by Johnie Winch. **Brighton's ninth folk club** opened on 7 October as *'Blues and*

Beyond' on Saturday evenings above the Kangaroo Coffee Lounge at 163 Western Road, Brighton. After just ten weeks it closed suddenly on 9 December.

This was followed, some eight months later, by another club with the same musical base, *'The Richmond Blues Club'*. Opening originally in Lewes on 6 August 1968 it transferred to the Richmond in Brighton after just five weeks because the support was so strong the club needed larger premises thus becoming **Brighton's tenth folk club**. It opened on 10 September with Jo Ann Kelly as the guest and Roger Hubbard, Nigel Manzel, Dick Wardell and Sam Mitchell as residents. It was however to be short-lived and closed suddenly on 12 November with a suggestion that it would reopen shortly. Just three weeks later on Wednesday 3 December it re emerged, with Roger Hubbard as the organiser, as a fortnightly club at the Prince George in Trafalgar Street where it finally closed on 8 April 1970.

Roger Hubbard *John Collyer*

Dick Wardell eventually re-appeared as a resident at the Lady Jane Blues and Contemporary folk club on Shoreham Beach in 1971. Vic Smith, writing in the Brighton and Hove Herald on 3 April noted

"Last summer, the Stanford Arms used to be the venue for a Saturday night country and western club, but this never really had enough support to make it financially viable, suggesting there is not enough room in Brighton for this specialist type of club. Now Roger Hubbard is finding the same thing with his country blues club which meets at the Prince George in Trafalgar Street. This Wednesday sees the last meeting of this club, but they have really decided to go out with a bang, for the guest for this meeting is Jo Ann Kelly, the foremost female blues singer in this country."

The next regular session was at The Gloucester, Gloucester Road meeting on Wednesday evenings it opened on 12 December 1968 with Sydney Carter – composer of 'Lord of the Dance' as the first guest. This club survived long enough to be recognised as **Brighton's eleventh folk club**. Organised by the husband and wife team of Vic and Tina [Christine] Smith, then newly arrived in the town, they were soon joined as residents by Lea Nicholson.

At the end of July 1969, because of building work and for one week only, the club transferred to the Stanford Arms then, from August, to a new 'permanent' home at The Prince George, Trafalgar Street. After four months it moved again and on 6 January 1970, with Diz Disley as guest and changing to Tuesday evenings, opened at The Marlborough, Princes Street where Terry Masterson replaced Lea as a resident.

Vic and Tina Smith
[right]
and
Lea Nicholson
[below].
both Jim Marshall

The story behind three venues in such a short space of time was described by Vic in the first issue of The Brighton Folk Diary and typifies the problems encountered by all club organisers at some time.

"The folk club starting at the 'Marlborough Hotel' in Pavilion Street will be our 3rd venture in this field in just over a year. We started in December 1968 at the 'Gloucester' on Wednesdays. This quickly became a well-supported club and was going from strength to strength when the decision to close the 'Gloucester' for radical alterations was taken. We were forced to move at the end of July to make way for a discotheque. We had lined up alternative premises in another pub, but the proposed move could not take place as this clubroom was also to be altered, this time into a restaurant. This meant a last minute search for premises, and we decided on the 'Prince George' in Trafalgar Street. In the four months that we have been there we have seen our audiences dwindle, and there can be no doubt that the elusive 'atmosphere' of the 'Gloucester' was not recaptured. This has led to another search and after looking at a good number of rooms, we have decided on the 'Marlborough'. This room is not available on Wednesdays, but rather than lose

what we think is potentially an excellent room we have decided to run the club on Tuesday nights."

A significant innovation was the regular introduction of traditional or source singers from outside Sussex as guest artistes. It was at the Prince George, on 8 October 1969 that the 72 year old Scottish former shepherd Willie Scott sang to a Brighton audience and a few months later, on 10 March 1970, in the Marlborough the superb Scottish singer Lizzie Higgins first appeared in the town.

There was, of course, a range of star guests but even these included the less common and included a rare club appearance in Sussex of Anne Briggs. Unfortunately this club closed at the end of April 1970 when it featured the superb local musical duo Robin Arzonie on fiddle and Derek Lockwood on accordion. Thankfully Vic and Tina were not deterred and went on to become major participants in the Sussex folk scene for the next three decades.

Peter Tiplady and Robin Arzonie.
Jim Marshall

During 1969 Vic and Tina also ran a free admission folk session. Initially in the Gloucester but when that venue became unavailable in July they continued the session until January 1970 in the Cartwheel Cellar Bar of Harrisons on the seafront.

On Saturdays and Tuesdays in 1969 it was possible to visit one of the most unusually named clubs in the country – *'Cuthbert Toad Hall'* – in the basement of the YWCA, Regency House, Oriental Place. Organised by Audrey Judd with the talented singer/guitarist and songwriter Pete Collins as resident, **Brighton's twelfth club** started on Saturday 29 November 1969 and quickly expanded to Tuesdays as well.

Not since the original Ballads and Blues club of 1961 had there been a club in unlicensed premises, a point Vic Smith noted in his weekly article in the Brighton and Hove Herald on 19 December 1969 when he wrote *"What is the minimum age for a folk enthusiast? It seems that nearly all clubs think that this is 18 as they meet on licensed premises where minors are not welcome. There must be a potential audience among younger, people and now a club has opened which demonstrates that this is the case. "We have 12, 13 and 14 year-olds coming along," says Audrey Judd, co-organiser of the Cuthbert Toad Hall Folk Club, which meets in Regency House YWCA in*

Oriental Place on Tuesdays and Saturdays. This does not mean that the club is aimed exclusively at these youngsters, for folk music is age-less in its character and appeal."

Saturday evenings featured a guest singer and during the first years these included Long John Baldry, Gordon Giltrap, Gerry Lockran, Diz Disley, Cliff Aungier, the Orange Blossom Sound, Vera Johnson and Wizz Jones. Later appearances were made by Bridget St John, Mike Marran, Joe Stead, Don and Sarah Morgan and Miles Wootton. Tuesday, on the other hand, was a local singer's night, initially with Pete but subsequently hosted by Keith and Cherry Meddings. Then, during June 1971, I became a resident at both evenings until they closed in September of that year.

Pete Collins.
Jim Marshall

Roger Brasier.
Jim Marshall

Briefly, from 16 January to 2 December 1970, there was a ***King and Queen Folk Club*** at, unsurprisingly, the King and Queen in Marlborough Place with Sussex University student Roger Brasier as compère. Roger, who was later to become a resident at Friday's Folk Club, was unusual in that he was not a singer. He relied instead, to great effect, on the spoken word with highly entertaining readings of prose and poetry ranging from melodramatic to witty and even ridiculous. As Vic Smith explained in the Mid Sussex Times on 12 August 1976 *"If I were to tell you that one of the most popular entertainers in local folk clubs doesn't sing and doesn't play an instrument, I would probably raise an eyebrow or two but this certainly is the case. Roger Brasier relies on his remarkable ability to interpret the written word to entertain. He has a huge repertoire of dramatic monologues, poems and silly ditties, and he can provide* *an entertaining evening with them. He first started coming around the local folk clubs about six years ago. At that time he was an undertaker and his comic poems were able to provide a little light relief from this. Since then he has shown how seriously he takes his poetry, by taking a very good degree in English at the University of Sussex. He will be going back to Falmer in September to do research."*

In its short life this club featured guests ranging from Allan 'Spud' Taylor, Diz Disley, Johnny Silvo, Derek Brimstone, Cliff Aungier, Gerry Lockran and Jo-Ann Kelly to Shirley Collins, Alex Campbell and The Yetties.

Once a month, on Sunday evenings, there was a session *'Guitar at the Marlborough'* in The Marlborough, Princes Street organised by John Thackeray and Michael Trory. This ran from 4 January 1971 to 4 February 1973.

Brighton Folk Diary No.7 for January and February 1971 noted that the "weekly sessions at Prinny's" were, from Tuesday 5 January 1971 moving to **Folk at the Arlington**, Marine Parade for what was to be one of the town's longer running folk sessions, although initially the day of the meetings varied. During the first eight weeks, five were on a Tuesday and there was one each on a Monday, Wednesday and Thursday with admission costing 2/- [10 pence]. It ran more as a mini concert and showcase for the residents with occasional spots for local singers rather than a club in the sense that other clubs had regular appearances of star guests.

Mike Trory. *Jim Marshall*

The resident group were the entertaining and highly popular Brighton Taverners (later The Taverners) originally comprising Andy Tunmer, Stuart Reed and Pete Cartlidge who had come together in 1967 as mature students at The College of Education at Falmer. Stuart had previously worked in the merchant navy with Cunard and the Blue Star Line, while Andy and Pete had been in the banking industry. Early in 1976, they were joined by Geoff Goater a former professional footballer. Apart from their own club they were popular and frequent guests at most of the local clubs since although they were, like many others in the folk world, employed as teachers during the day they spent most of their leisure time singing. The first of several long-playing albums 'Wrap it up for the Lady' was released on the Sussex based 'Long Man' record company in May 1976 and to celebrate

30 years of performing Stuart, Pete and Geoff, together with Paul Downes and Will Southcote-Want released a CD 'Still Rolling' in 1996.

Vic Smith noted in the Mid Sussex Times on 19 February 1976 *"The most popular and hard-working group is undoubtedly the Taverners from Brighton. Although the group operates on a semi-professional basis, it seems to be working most nights of the week throughout London and the south-east. They make three appearances in the area this week, including a local one at the Fox and Hounds Folk Club, Fox Hill, Haywards Heath, on Sunday night. ...The key factor in their success seems to be versatility. They have a broad appeal, a huge repertoire of songs, three excellent voices which blend together well, and appealing personalities."*

'The Taverners':
Andy Tunmer, Stuart Reed and
Pete Cartlidge.
The Taverners

The club continued at The Arlington until June 1973. During the summer of 1971 the demand for folk was so high that they met twice a week on Tuesday and either Friday or Saturday evenings. On 8 May 1973, Ted Potter the landlord of the Pier Hotel introduced his own folk club on Tuesday evenings. A month later, on 5 June, the Taverners moved out of the Arlington while building works were carried out and took over the Tuesday night sessions at the Pier. In September there was a suggestion they would move back to the Arlington, renamed The Hungry Years, but this didn't materialise and they remained at the Pier for a further eight months.

In May 1974 they transferred to The Buccaneer. Pete Cartlidge left in the autumn of 1977 but the group continued at this venue until Christmas 1979 before moving on to The Concorde, Marine Drive in February 1980 – this time on Monday evenings.

This was probably the only commercially viable folk session since there were no guest fees to be paid and performing, as it did, regularly to large audiences, particularly at Easter and during the summer months when it was a major attraction for the annual 'invasion' of students from all corners of Europe. Nevertheless as general interest in folk declined it closed in September 1981 after ten years of regular weekly meetings.

The annual summer influx of foreign students mentioned earlier, although initially welcomed by club organisers right across the region for their economic value, eventually proved less attractive since they packed the club rooms to such an extent that some regulars stayed away during the summer months. Then, against a background of what Vic Smith described as "an, assault by the extreme right wing Thatcher led government on virtually all performing arts that failed to fit into market dominated policies – jazz, fringe theatre and specialist music", general interest declined. Many of the early enthusiasts lost the habit of attending the clubs on a weekly basis and audience numbers dropped. The Taverners however, to cater specifically for the summer demands of the annual

student invasion, reopened their sessions at Easter 1982 [29 March to 12 April] and again in the summer of that year [from June until the end of September]. This formula was repeated for the next four years; in 1983 [21 March to 18 April and 6 June to the end of August], 1984 [9 to 23 April and 12 June to the end of August], 1985 [25 March to 8 April and 10 June to 19 August] and finally 1986 [24 and 31 March and 16 June to the end of August].

Stuart Reed c1996. *Jim Marshall*

Much earlier, in July 1976, Stuart Reed summarised the situation in the Folk Diary No.40 SOAPBOX

"This is the season when the Sussex clubs, particularly those along the coast, find their audiences swelled considerably with holidaymakers. And in most clubs they are very welcome. But perhaps welcome is not the right word. Tolerated maybe, especially if the visitors are from abroad. Because, like it or not, these bronzed, T-shirted, carefree bearers of healthy currencies don't take the English folk revival as seriously as we do. The result is that, at our Tuesday club at the Buccaneer for instance, many of the native regulars simply stay away until the season is over. And the same tale is heard all the way from Eastbourne to Torquay.
Alright, so a group of foreigners can be a disruptive element in a club; but then, most guests and even floor singers, treat their audience to what might objectively be called a lecture/recital, and they're just not used to it. Mind you, it should be admitted that even ostensibly knowledgeable audiences become restive when the most revered of performers delve into less melodic and familiar material. And Bob Copper is quick to scotch the romantic notion that his father or grandfather had only to sing the first bars of "Claudy Banks" and the whole village joined in. Sometimes they'd say, "There goes that Jim Copper with his daft songs again". At other times, when the mood was right, they'd sing along

and have a knees up. That's as it should be. And that's the spirit that the
Germans and Swedes and all bring – to our club at least.

It's often asked why these people trouble to come to folk clubs at all, since
most of what goes on must be unintelligible. The answer is that in the whole
of western Europe Britain is the only place where the oral tradition is still
flourishing: the French chansons are now only concert-hall pieces; in
Germany nobody wants to sing Volkslieder since Hitler annexed them to his
master-race propaganda; Flamenco is for tourists, and the Scandinavians
never had any in the first place. That's why they're so enthusiastic, and its
effect is a rejuvenating one, and much needed.

So let's share our heritage with the rest of Europe. Extend the hand of
friendship – at this time of year it'll be crossed with silver. There's always a
silver lining – even on the most cynical horizon."

This was not quite the end of the Taverners though as one regular feature
had been their Christmas Party and these enduring events are still held each
year. Although Andy Tunmer died in 1992 the group, with a revised personnel
which still includes Stuart Reed and Geoff Goater and from time to time Pete
Cartlidge, continue to perform today although now mainly for barn dances.
From the early days Stuart always combined group work with solo appearances,
a fervent supporter of virtually all of the local clubs, he appeared at various
times as a resident at the Sunday Club, the Monday Club, Brighton Singers Club
and Copper Folk at Peacehaven. Today he continues to pursue his solo career
although now rarely in folk clubs, often singing instead in Irish bars.

Earlier there was a brief folk session at Jimmy's in Steine Street starting
on 30 July 1971 but no further details are recorded. Two months later in
September a "soft music club" but not necessarily folk, run by Paul Carpenter
opened at the Imperial in Queens Road but the pub was sold and it closed
after one week before re-appearing a month later at the Richmond Hotel,
Richmond Place. Again there are no further details recorded and it would
appear to have been short-lived.

In the autumn of 1971 on alternate Tuesdays, starting 7 October, folk once
more appeared – although but briefly – at The Marlborough, Princes Street
organised by John Bassett [also known as John Zarfass] and Indrani. The last
advertised date for these sessions was 16 December 1971. There was mention,
in 1972, by Jim Marshall in his newspaper report of a club on Wednesday
evenings at the Polytechnic. A later advertisement was in the name of *'Polyfolk'*
on 22 March 1979 at Sallis Benney Hall, Grand Parade while a week earlier on
16 March Vic Smith, writing in the Mid Sussex Times, reported *"A third*
Thursday club does not meet regularly throughout the year. The Poly Folk Club
at Brighton polytechnic's Sallis Benney Hall meets only during term time but
will be there next Thursday meeting with the very popular folk comedian Fred
Wedlock from Bristol." Later that year, on 5 October, Vic reported in the same

paper that Bob Fox and Stu Luckley were appearing at the Brighton Poly Folk Club.

Regular Monday folk 'sessions' started at the Hanbury Arms, Kemp Town in March 1973 and on 21 May with Alan White as guest became a formal club organised by Tim Broadbent, Miles Wootton and Laurie Goddard. The venture was, however, short-lived and closed on 11 June. July 1974 saw the introduction of a second folk night at the Buccaneer with a contemporary trio 'Romany' in residence on Thursday evenings but this appears to have been another short lived session and was mentioned for only a few weeks by Jim Marshall in the Brighton and Hove Gazette. At about the same time – from 25 May until 10 August 1973 – on Friday nights I was involved as compère for a late night 'session' held in the Liaison Club, a charity café for the elderly run by Local Aid, in West Street. These featured a number of local singers and started at 11.00pm, running through until about 1.30am.

During the summer of 1974, on Thursday 20 June with Jo-Ann Kelly as opening guest, a new *'Brighton Ballads and Blues'* club was opened by Nick Burdett in the King and Queen, Marlborough Place. Despite an excellent line up of guests including Wizz Jones, Alan White, Peter Bellamy, Davy Graham, Joe Locker, Lea Nicholson, Tony Rose, Nic Jones, Tom Paley and Alistair Anderson this club, like many others, also had a short life and after closing for Christmas on 19 December of the same year failed to re-open.

September 1976 saw the opening of regular twice-weekly sessions of folk music in the bar of The Shakespeare's Head on Thursday and Sunday evenings. Although not a folk club these proved very durable and lasted for some years. Soon after these sessions started another new club – *'Super Folk'* – organised by Steve Baker and specialising in contemporary folk song, opened at The Queens Park Tavern, Queens Road. Commencing on Friday 5 November 1976, the following year, on 23 February, as *'Folk on 42nd'*, it changed to Wednesday evenings and closed on 29 June 1977.

Now to two interlinked sessions that have become the most durable of the later clubs in the town. In 1976 Eric Meadows, Andy Turner and Maxine Bennett, three teachers at Saltdean Middle School along with Doug Loveridge from the local church formed the group 'Cloudesley Shovell' – a name taken from Admiral Sir Cloudesley Shovell who allegedly anchored the British fleet off the Sussex coast so that he could be rowed ashore to visit his mother in Hastings - performing initially at the school but later at local events. This was before the decline in interest in folk and with encouragement from The Taverners they decided to organise a folk club. This they duly did and on the 28 February 1977 held their first session in the upstairs room of The King and Queen, Marlborough Place with John Copper and a local duo Chesterfield as guests. Unfortunately there was a live jazz band downstairs and the two were clearly incompatible so they quickly transferred to the Marlborough, Princes

Street as *'The Monday Folk Club'* opening there on 14 March with Miles Wootton as the first guest.

Eric Meadows. *Eric Meadows*

Supported initially by Stuart Reed they were joined as residents in February 1978 by myself, in the summer by Jane White and in December of that year by Fiona and Don Watts. The weekly guests were mostly locally based singers but the few exceptions included Tony Rose, Nic Jones, Chris Foster, Roy Harris and Dave Goulder. On 4 April 1979 the Monday Club changed days and became *'The Wednesday Folk Club'* where changes to the residents included the introduction of Christine Hase in August of that year.

[left]
Fiona Watts [née Gibson] *and* *[right]* **Don Watts** *Both John Collyer*

Next year saw the introduction of Joy Ansell, Tony Toole and Donna Chatfield along with the American Pete Durgerian as additional residents and major guests booked during this period were Martin Wyndham-Read, The Amazing Mr Smith, Leon Rosselson, Martin Carthy, Johnny Coppin, Bill Caddick, Pete and Chris Coe and Cyril Tawney.

Briefly for a few weeks in early June 1980 there were two sessions running on Wednesday evenings with a formal club upstairs in the clubroom and an informal sing-around session downstairs in the bar. Towards the end of 1980 as other commitments increased Eric, whilst remaining a resident, handed the organising over to me. Early in 1981 the residents were, in addition to Eric and myself, Don and Fiona Watts, Christine Hase, Donna Chatfield, Gordon Allen, Lesley Smith and Barry Walker. Soon after the sessions were transferred to the bar as singarounds and Eric dropped out of the residency while I handed the organising over to the duo, Indrani and Martin Shough.

Meanwhile in the autumn of 1978, on Saturday 7 October with Johnny Doughty as guest I, aided by Eric as co-host, opened *'The Brighton Singers Club'* also at The Marlborough.

BRIGHTON SINGERS CLUB

FOLK SONG AND MUSIC

7·45 pm EVERY SATURDAY

THE MARLBOROUGH

PRINCES ST., OLD STEINE

sing play or listen.

Clive Bennett Jerry Jordan

Eric Meadows Stuart Reed

Eddie Upton Fiona Watts

Brighton Singers Club poster 1978.
The author

Christine Hase. *Jim Marshall*

Lesley Smith [standing] & Tony Hobden.
Jim Marshall

This introduced to Brighton the first radical change in style of presentation since the first club on Sunday afternoons some seventeen years earlier in September 1961. The club aim was to provide a venue for traditional song and music and this was emphasised by bi-monthly guest booking of traditional singers. Instead of the audience sitting in rows facing a focal point which each artiste occupied in turn as they performed, the seating was arranged round tables which were set out in a large open circle and, passing round the circle, everybody present was invited in turn to perform a single item before the turn moved on. Similar in style to the original Horsham Songswappers in 1960. This was varied slightly when there was a guest singer for the evening who would be asked to perform a set of three pieces before the turn passed on its way. In March 1979 Eric was forced by other commitments to drop out and was replaced as co-host by Fiona Watts who had been one of the club 'regulars'. Instead of residents the club had initiated 'regulars' who initially, in addition to Fiona, included Stuart Reed, Jerry Jordan and Eddie Upton to which were added later Christine Hase and briefly Sandra Goddard.

Early guests included Clare Clayton, Tony Foxworthy, Roy Harris, Shirley Collins and Claire Ross-Watkins, a mountain dulcimer player from the USA. By the end of the year Stuart, Jerry, Eddie and Sandra had all left and been replaced by Dave Fisher, Ed Ford and Martin and Indrani Shough.

The following year [1980], as the landlord expanded the use of the clubroom with other organisations, the club was gradually transferred from the upstairs room down to the bar. Fiona left and sometime later, she and Don having decided to go their separate ways, reverted to her maiden name of Fiona Gibson. Meanwhile I had handed over the organising of this club as well as the Wednesday Folk Club to Indrani and Martin supported at first by Barry Walker, Lesley Smith, Ian Fyvie, Jim Daniels, Alan 'Woody' Woodham, and Alex Daguerre to which were later added Brian Faulkner and Dave Fisher. In 1982 the club advertisement in Folk Diary No. 74 recorded "with sadness" the "passing of fellow resident and good friend Brian Faulkner" on 19 February. Probably best remembered for his unique 'Ryebuck Shearer', this talented interpreter of working men's songs will be sorely missed."

Martin and Indrani Shough
Jim Marshall

In 1988 Folk Diary No.112 recorded *"Congratulations to Brighton singer/songwriter, Indrani, on winning the Oxfam national "Only One Of" competition. Her song "Don't throw*

65

It all Away" gained her the prize for the most original entry. Indrani has had a long association with the singarounds at the Marlborough Hotel in Brighton, but she recently handed the organisation of the Saturday sessions over to Kluggers.". In fact the sessions were by then, and still are today, organised by Ian Fyvie assisted by John 'Kluggers the Barred' McCluskey.

These 'Free Singaround' sessions continued, twice a week, in the bar until December 1991 when they transferred to The Stable [now renamed the Babalabar], Albion Street where they endured, still on Wednesday and Saturday evenings, until November 1997.

Ian Fyvie *Jim Marshall*   **John 'Kluggers' McCluskey [left] with Ian Fyvie**
    John McCluskey

Dave Fisher *Dave Fisher*

The club's organisers were by then well aware of their long unbroken sequence of meetings. When it became necessary to move from the Stable, since a new venue was not immediately available, rather than close they found a temporary home at The Battle of Waterloo in Rock Place before transferring, in February 1998, to The Jolly Brewer in Ditchling Road. At the same time they ended the Saturday sessions and settled on Wednesday evenings for weekly meetings. Eighteen months later, in October 1999, they relocated to The Hollingbury in Hollingdean then, in 2000, to The George Beard [formerly

The Eagle], in Gloucester Road where Brighton's first singaround sessions were held in 1961. In June 2001 the meetings, now called **Brighton Singers' Folk Club**, moved to the Prestonville Arms in Hamilton Road, still once a week on a Wednesday and now, with twenty-two years' continuous presentation of folk music, ranked as the third longest running club in the area.

In 1987 under the heading 'Brighton's Longest Running Singaround' the Wednesday evenings became for a few weeks, theme sessions with titles like 'Cruel Wars', 'Sixties', 'Fantasy' and 'Railways' with various hosts including Fred Baxter, Jill Hockmuth and Colin Baker, Mark Worledge, Ian Fyvie and Indrani while the Saturday evenings remained more traditional and were hosted by John 'Kluggers' McCluskey and Julie Hall.

It was not long however before they reverted to their general broad based sing-around format offering a forum for traditional folk, blues, country and western, contemporary song and even acoustic 'pop' music.

As mentioned earlier in relation to the Taverners, by the end of the 70's the folk boom was on the wane and over the next two years several new ventures proved not to be viable and closed almost as soon as they opened:

• Folk returned briefly to The Eagle, Gloucester Road on Sunday evenings from February to March 1979 with a contemporary club – *'Folk at The Eagle'*. Organised by Bob Gibson with Dave Langridge, Paul Reynolds and Steve Hall as residents. Vic Smith noted in the Mid Sussex Times on 1 February 1979 *"Brighton now has two folk clubs on a Sunday night, another one having recently been formed to meet at the Eagle in Gloucester Road. This club has got off to a very promising start and, as so often happens with a new folk club, the floor singers that have been attracted to it have not been heard in other folk clubs in the area. The general standard of the singing here has been promisingly high, and in Dave Langridge they have a lively compère and talented resident singer."*

• Wilbury Jam, a broad based folk entertainment group first got together in the spring of 1976. Over the next three years they developed a unique act comprising comedy songs, ballads and items requiring audience participation while continuing to play in pubs, social clubs and folk clubs around Sussex. Then – emulating The Taverners – they opened regular sessions in the Concorde Bar, Marine Drive on alternate Wednesday evenings commencing 1 August 1979. By the following summer these had become weekly meetings and in October 1980 they changed the day to a Sunday and ran until July 1981. Once their Concorde sessions closed they continued performing, but mainly concert venues.

This entertaining multi instrumental trio, comprised Nick Forrest, lead vocals, guitar, ukulele, recorder and mandolin; Mike Wood, guitar, banjo, violin, mandolin, clarinet and vocals and Pete Callaghan, double bass, accordion and vocals. Early in the 1980's Peter moved back to his ancestral roots in Solihull which extended the group area and they were soon working around the West Midlands as well as Sussex. In addition to their band work all three members are heavily involved in music. Pete plays in a symphony orchestra and encourages interest in music and the arts at the school of which he is head master. Mike, is Head of Expressive Arts Faculty at Oakmeads School, Burgess Hill and Musical Director and Conductor of the local choral society, and Nick who is Head of Performing Arts at Fonthill Lodge School, has sung many lead roles with the locally based Heber Opera. It was at the Concorde that they

recorded their LP record "A Good Spread" released in February 1981 followed in 1990 by "A Second Helping".

**Wilbury Jam.
Pete Callaghan,
Mike Wood and
Nick Forrest.**
Mike Wood

• Raffles Wine Bar in St James Street was the home for the ***'Brighton Troubadours Club'***, described as a club meeting *". . in an informal atmosphere and providing the best in amplified local folk music, jazz and blues."* on alternate Mondays from 22 September 1980 to 23 March 1981 featuring, among others, Pete Durgerian and Barry Walker, Jim Daniels, Warwick Downes and Martyn Bradley and The Exiles – Nick Burbridge, Dave Flewett and Rosie Short.

During the winter of 1981/2 folk song was to be heard virtually every night at Raffles with John Zarfass performing on Tuesday, Wednesday and Saturday; 'Alien Dream' [Indrani and Martin] and Ian Fyvie on Friday and a 'Folk Night' on Thursday featuring Indrani and Martin, Ian Fyvie, Brian and Margaret Dowdall, Dave Fisher, Brian Faulkner and Barry Walker.

• ***'Live Music at The Rainbow'*** – one of the largest regular folk sessions ever held in the town, opened on a once a month basis in The Rainbow Room of The Brighton Centre on Saturday 4 October 1980 with Alan White, Tim Broadbent, Christine Hase, Pete Durgerian and Don and Fiona Watts as residents. In January 1981 the sessions transferred to The Concorde Bar, Marine Parade but once more, despite an impressive guest list including Bert Jansch for the opening night followed by Jo Anne Kelly, Brian Cookman, Richard Digance and Fred Wedlock, even this bold venture was short lived and closed on 4 July 1981 with Roaring Jelly.

•   On Saturday 24 October 1981 there was a 'Come All Ye' session, organised jointly by The Springfield and Stanford folk clubs together with the Lewes Arms club, at The Old Market Arts Centre in Hove. This was followed by a second session on 19 December with 'Hope in the Valley' providing a Christmas flavour. This informal folk 'choir' was formed by a group of local singers and musicians to perform old Christmas carols which had either been collected from, or survived in the manuscripts of Sussex village singers and musicians.

•   Also in October 1981 folk song sessions started in the bar of The Pedestrians, Foundry Street featuring Don Watts and Dave Jenkin

•   and then, on Wednesday evenings early in 1982 singarounds started in the bar of the Royal Oak, St James Street featuring Don Watts, John Collyer, Stuart Reed, Dave Jenkin and John Bickford. Terry Masterson was a visitor to one of these sessions and was approached by Frank MacMahon of the nearby Le Café de Paris who suggested he might open a folk music club in the cosy basement of the pub. Terry was a little reluctant, fearing the heyday of formal folk clubs had passed and that it would be difficult to successfully sustain such a session but was eventually persuaded. As Terry put it "The room was undoubtedly good and Frank's powers of persuasion even better – well, he is Irish!"

Frank MacMahon and Terry Masterson.
Terry Masterson

Terry decided that if Oak Apple Day and the 6 March were both on a Saturday that year he'd take a chance. This superstitious reason was based on the fact that all three previous ventures, including the long running Pug 'O Junch had started on that date. So it was that on Saturday 6 March 1982 a formal weekly club opened as *'Folk at the Oak'* organised by Terry Masterson together with administrative help from Chris Littledale, a well known restorer of tin toys, and Mike McRory-Wilson. Guest for the first night was the ever-popular Tim Broadbent.

Soon after opening there was a brief attempt by Terry to re-introduce Keith Johns to the local scene but by then, as mentioned earlier, he was showing the first signs of multiple sclerosis. This affected his ability to hear if he was in tune and with this handicap Keith effectively retired from singing. The early omens for the fledgling club were good but it soon became apparent that the landlord had expectations that were too high for that time in the evolution of the folk movement and with increasing conflict between him and the club the organisers 'threw the towel in' and closed the venture during July.

Chris Littledale. *Tim Kent*

Singaround style seemed to be the answer to falling attendances and in February 1984 Jim Marshall and Eddie Upton opened a weekly session on Monday evenings in The Queens Head, Steine Street but by late September of that year this also closed.

There is mention in the Folk Diary No. 92 for April/May 1985 of *"NEW BRIGHTON CLUB. The Regency Folk Club recently opened on Monday nights at the Queen's Head in Steine Street, Brighton".* Since the copy date would have been late February it would appear likely that this club was running in March 1985 but it seems to have had a very short existence as there is no further mention of it.

Then, at about the same time, Tim Kent, supported by Antony Hodgson and Bob Howlett, opened a singaround folk club on Tuesday evenings and on 12 March 1985, just five days after the long running Friday's Folk closed, *'Noblefolk'* was born in Noble's Wine Bar, New Road. There was no admission charge, instead Tim adopted a system of 'fines' ranging from 10 to 20 pence for such 'sins' as forgetting words, using prompt notes, borrowing an instrument, breaking a string or using swear words. A more substantial 'fine' of £1 was levied for singing hackneyed songs such as Wild Rover or Streets of London. The sessions proved immensely popular, attracting a host of local singers week after week to the small upstairs bar where they were held until February 1986 after which the club moved first to The Queens Head, Steine Street and then on 4 March to Nash's Hotel, Marine Parade.

This also proved a short stay and in December 1986 it transferred back to Nobles Wine Bar where in the autumn of 1989 the Folk Diary reported *"NOBLEFOLK is on the move after a change of management at Nobles Wine Bar in Brighton and Tim and Val Kent are currently trying to arrange another venue for these popular weekly singarounds. A change of day is likely as well as Tim is becoming involved in the team that produces the BBC Radio Sussex folk music programme "Minstrel's Gallery", which is recorded on Tuesday evenings".*

The change of venue did not take place but the sessions moved to Thursday evenings until finally closing in September 1990, by when the venue had been renamed Mrs Fitzherbert's. By then also, the club's system of fines had raised some £2,500, which was used to provide two dogs for the Sussex Branch of Guide Dogs for the Blind and a video recorder for deaf people in Kemptown.

In October, as Nobles Folk closed, Tim Kent took over running 'Folk at The Elephant' in Lewes until February 1993 when he transferred back to Brighton with **'Hanbury Folk'** at The Hanbury Arms, Paston Place, Kemp Town, which closed on 29 December 1993. By that time Tim Kent and Ivor George had formed a duo, known in 1992 as 'The Ferrets' and from 1993 as 'Two and a Hat'. Together they performed a wide range of folk material.

Tim Kent *Tim Kent*

In January 1986 the **'Bright Helm Stone'** folk club opened on Thursday evenings at Doctor Brightons' Kings Road but by August that year had moved to The Prince Albert, Trafalgar Street with Ainneagh O'Reagan-King and Jethro as residents, subsequently joined by Antony Hodgson. In March 1987 this had become another singaround club, meeting in the bar rather than the clubroom and finally closed in March 1988.

Folk returned briefly to The Springfield Hotel, Springfield Road on the 13 April 1988. First with a song and tune session run by Sandra Goddard from April until 10 August on the second Wednesday of each month and then, every Thursday from 6 October until early in 1989 with the **'Springfield Music Nights'**, a mixture of music, dance and song. Issue 115 of the Folk Diary for February and March 1989 noted *"The impending departure from this area of Brendan and Chrissie Buckley has brought to an end the Thursday night song and dance evening at the Springfield Hotel which they ran with Vic and Christine Smith."*

A key element in this revival of folk at the Springfield was the return to Brighton from the Thatched Inn at Keymer of Heather and Jim Keelty, the popular landlady and landlord who had been such an important part of the Friday's Folk success during the 1970's.

The next venue for folk was Hangleton Manor Hotel, Hangleton Valley Drive, Hove – the oldest inhabited building in Brighton and Hove [dating from 1540] where *'Folk at The Manor'* ran on the fourth Thursday of each month from April 1988 to 23 July 1992 with the group Broadstone as residents.

Another brief venture *'Folk at the Racehill'* was at The Racehill Inn, Lewes Road on Tuesday evenings organised by John Hayward. Although it ran only from 25 September 1990 to March 1991, during this time it featured an early appearance of traditional singer Ron Spicer and regular visits from Bob Lewis. Bob was originally from the West Sussex village of Heyshott but eventually settled in Saltdean. He started singing at the Chichester folk club and later danced with the Martlett Morris Men and over the final two decades of the twentieth century earned himself a reputation as an excellent singer of traditional songs.

Bob Lewis at Co-op Folk Day, Brighton Dressed in Martlett Morris kit. *Jim Marshall*

Over the years Brighton has been popular with street buskers and several were regular performers in the folk clubs. One of the most accomplished was Alan 'Woodie' Woodham with material ranging from folk to pop songs. Another well known character and busker, although less flexible in his music, being a long time devotee of 'Leadbelly' and the blues, was Jim Daniels who accompanied himself on a big 12 string guitar.

Jim Daniels *Tim Kent*

The last song club to be organised in Brighton before the new millennium was the *'Wizard Folk Club'*, meeting in the Prince Albert,

Trafalgar Street on Tuesday evenings from April 1995 to January 1996. Organised by Tim Kent with Paul Holden, Mike Dixon, Miles Wootton, John Collyer and Dave Earl as residents. Admission was free and there were occasional guests, including Les Barker for the final night.

John Collyer. *John Collyer*   **'Woodie' Woodham.** *Tim Kent*

Four years later, on 5 December 2000, Tim Kent and John Collyer – former resident at the Sunday, Stanford Arms, folk club – opened a new Brighton club *'Folk / Blues and Beyond'* meeting on the first Tuesday of each month in the downstairs room of the Schooner Inn, Southwick. The club policy was to feature occasional top name guest from a broad folk 'entertainment' base.

With so many clubs and top quality singers over the years it is not too surprising that the influence of the Brighton folk scene was felt in the surrounding towns. The surprising thing is just how deeply the development of other early clubs in the surrounding area was a result of the pioneers of the 'revival' in Brighton and no record of the Brighton scene would be complete without some acknowledgement of this.

The easy relationship between 'rival' clubs and the social friendships made in these settings ran on in to other areas. One associated activity to benefit was Morris dancing and the Worthing based Chanctonbury Ring Morris Men's club counted among its members at various times, Paul Setford, Eddie Upton, Tim Broadbent, Vic Smith and Jerry Jordan.

4 EXPANSION INTO THE SURROUNDING AREA

WORTHING

The earliest town affected by the developing Brighton folk scene was Worthing. Forced to find a new venue for our Ballads and Blues Club by the loss to summer trade of Melbray's Restaurant in Brighton, Terry Scarlett and I transferred nearer our homes in West Sussex and from 26 March to 24 September 1962 organised the *'Worthing Ballads and Blues Club'*, meeting on Monday evenings at The Railway Hotel in Chapel Road. The choice of town was partly prompted by the number of people from Worthing who regularly travelled to Brighton to listen to folk music assuring us of a reasonable audience at the new location.

The Southern Folk Music Society
PRESENTS

FOLK NIGHT

at the Worthing Ballads & Blues Club

THE RAILWAY HOTEL

Chapel Road :: Worthing
(2 MINUTES FROM CENTRAL STATION)

Every MONDAY 8 to 10.15 p.m.

★ REGULAR APPEARANCE OF LONDON ARTISTES ★

Membership 1/-   Admission 2/6

Enquiries: T. SCARLETT :: 89 FIRCROFT CRESCENT :: RUSTINGTON :: SUSSEX

Southern Folk Music Society poster 1962 *The author*

The club was again organised in the name of The Southern Music Society by Terry and myself although, during the summer, Terry left to take up a new job in Bristol and his last performance on the local scene was on Monday 13 August.

The supporting residents were the other members of The Beachcombers – Bob McDonald and Valerie Greenfield, who was also a dancer with The Worthing Grasshopper folk dance club.

For the opening night Hilda Syms and Russell Quaye were booked and arrived with several singing 'friends' including Alex Campbell and Colin Wilkie. Although clubs were becoming more folk orientated Skiffle was still acceptable and Hilda and Russell's group reflected that with a one string bass using a barrel instead of a tea chest, a washboard and a home made 'wind' instrument. The Worthing Herald's report on Friday 30 March 1962 said:

"BALLADS AND BLUES FOR WORTHING
Among those who attended the informal opening of Worthing Ballads and Blues Club in the hall at the rear of the Railway Hotel on Monday evening was folk singer Alex Campbell.

After singing the lighthearted "Come for a ride in my car" he closed his short performance with a deeply moving item "Freedom," as sung by the Alabama negroes.

Also present was the husband and wife team, Hilda Syms and Russell Quay, who organised one of the first permanent folk clubs in London and formed the City Ramblers Group. They now have their own club in Dulwich.

Hilda, in a series of solos, ranged in her songs from Cockney humour to a spiritual "Two little fishes and five loaves of bread."

This local effort has come about through a highly successful season in Brighton of a parent club which built up a membership of 520, nearly 200 of whom came from the Worthing area."

Opening night at Worthing Ballads and Blues Club. *Front row,right* **Paul Morris, founder of Chichester Folk Club.** *Third row, Second left* **Jim Marshall.** *Second right, by window,* **Alex Campbell** *The author*

The Beachcombers at Worthing Ballads and Blues Club 11 June 1962 *[left to right:]* **the author, Bob McDonald, Valerie Greenfield and Terry Scarlett.** *The author*

In its brief life this club featured among others, Colin Wilkie and Shirley Hart and Fred Gerlach, the American 12-string guitarist.

With the departure of Terry the Southern Folk Music Society which we had founded needed to be restructured. I was left with full control and financial liability when Terry withdrew his share of the capital and became instead an

Honorary Vice President. Our final joint decision was to offer a similar title to Tony Wales, which he accepted.

A year later, in June 1963, when I closed the Brighton Ballads and Blues club I opted for a summer break rather than returning to Worthing. Four years elapsed before there was another attempt at establishing a folk song venue in the town and it was again to be Brighton based performers that took the initiative. This was *'The Troubadours'*, which started on 6 March 1966 with weekly session on Sunday evenings at The Malsters in Broadwater and was the brainchild of Jack Whyte, encouraged by the success of his other two ventures, Friday's Folk in Brighton and Pug O' Junch in Lewes. Here however he was joined in the organising by Terry Masterson and Miles Wootton.

Terry Masterson *[right] and*
Miles Wootton *[below]*
Both Jim Marshall

Unlike the other ventures, at Jack's insistence, they set out to run the Worthing club with no guest singers relying instead on the residents and floor singers. Experience proved this not to be the most practicable way and guest singers were introduced.

Initially this club was, like the other two, successful but possibly because it was some way from the town centre audiences started to decline and it survived for only one year.

On Monday evenings in the following year [1968] informal sessions organised by students from the West Sussex College of Art – led by Sarah Meynell and Sid Garner – started at The Fountain, Chapel Road.

After a short period, as the sessions became more formal, this became **Worthing Folk Club**, the town's third club and on 16 December once more came under the influence of the Brighton scene when I, having become a regular performer at the club after returning to the area from Kent, was invited to act as compère/host.

Southern Folk Music Society poster 1971
The author

Soon afterwards I took over the running of the club, once again in the name of the Southern Folk Music Society and quickly recruited additional resident singers being joined first by 'Whispering' Bob McDonald and later Bryan Blanchard and then, in February 1971, Don and Sarah Morgan.

The Southern Folk Music Society
PRESENTS
WORTHING FOLK CLUB'S

FOLK NIGHT

EVERY MONDAY AT 8 P.M.

in

THE FOUNTAIN HOTEL

CHAPEL ROAD, WORTHING

Membership 2/6   Admission 2/6

Enquiries — C. Bennett, The Gables, High Street, Angmering

Bryan Blanchard *Jim Marshall*

Don and Sarah Morgan at Worthing folk club *The author*

The club cultivated an impressive list of guest singers featuring Nic Jones, Shirley Collins, Martyn Wyndham-Read, Dave and Toni Arthur, John Foreman, Bob and John Copper and one of the great characters of the folk scene the Reverend Kenneth Loveless, Rural Dean of East Hackney, singer, concertina player and one time squire of The Morris Ring.

Meetings continued on Monday evenings until 8 June 1969 when they changed to Sundays for three weeks after which I closed the club due to work commitments, which kept me in Kent for six months. Returning to Sussex at the end of the year I reopened the club, reverting to Mondays, on 29 December 1969 still at The Fountain and with Martyn Wyndham-Read as the guest. Eventually, in July 1971, the club moved to The Norfolk, Chapel Road continuing there on Monday evenings until finally closing on 24 October 1973. To date this has been the longest running folk club in the town, surviving for virtually five years.

The major Worthing folk club since then has been *'The Southdown Folk Club'*, Northcourt Road, which opened on Thursday evenings in February 1974 with Andrew and Jane Dickson and Pete Logan as residents. This became *'Worthing Folk Club'* meeting at the Downsview Hotel, Downsview Road on 2 January 1975 before transferring to The Wine Lodge, Marine Parade in the summer of 1977 where the last advertised night was 31 October 1977

This was followed briefly in May to August 1979 by a Monday club in The Denton Lounge (Worthing Pier) with Jane Dickson as resident. Not until the new millennium did folk song return to Worthing wl. n Hilary Cook and Jenny Mercer opened *'What the Dickens'* a monthly Acoustic/Roots/Folk session meeting on Friday evenings in the Charles Dickens pub in Heene Road. By then most of the earlier venues had evolved - The Railway had been renamed the Lennox and featured karaoke evenings, the Fountain had received a make-over into a super pub called 'The Assembly' while the Norfolk had become the Area 51 Nightclub.

SHOREHAM BY SEA

In the autumn of 1963 Shoreham was the second of the surrounding towns to be colonised by the growing folk movement in Brighton. As mentioned in Chapter 2, after a summer break I opened the first *'Shoreham Folk Song Club'*, again in the name of The Southern Folk Music Society. This club met weekly on Tuesday evenings as 'Folk Night' in the clubroom of The Burrell Arms, Brunswick Road, Shoreham.

The opening night was 29 October with Alex Campbell as guest and floor singers included Paul Setford, Harry Mousdell and the traditional singer Bob Blake of Shipley.

The choice of Shoreham was due to several factors. This was still a time when many people had conventional ideas about the weekend including a visit to a dance on Saturday evening and the cinema on Sunday. In addition most young people relied on public transport, the era where every family owned a car was still some way off. I lived near Littlehampton and decided not to open in Brighton on a Sunday in competition with Johnie Winch's club but to seek a venue elsewhere for mid-week. I was faced with finding a clubroom that was both suitable and not too expensive to hire as well as being located somewhere accessible for folk enthusiasts from both Brighton and Worthing.

The Burrell Arms met all those criteria. The room was a useful size, the fee reasonable and the landlady sympathetic. It was also only minutes from the station and the times of late trains to both Worthing and Brighton were ideal.

Alex Campbell and the author performing at the opening night of Shoreham Folk Club.
A youthful Paul Setford in the front row.
The author

Meanwhile I had again restructured The Southern Folk Music Society. Alex Campbell had accepted an invitation to become President with Terry Scarlett and Tony Wales still Honorary Vice Presidents and myself as Chairman.

Southern Folk Music Society poster 1963
The author

Three weeks after the opening, with Shirley Collins as guest and much to the audience's delight, Alex Campbell also arrived just for a floor spot. He was booked to appear at the University Folk Club in Brighton the following night and as he had a free evening came to Shoreham for, as he said, "It is the only club where I am the President. Hell yeah!".

The Southern Folk Music Society

PRESENTS

FOLK NIGHT

at the Shoreham Folk Song Club

THE BURRELL ARMS

Brunswick Road, Shoreham

Every TUESDAY at 8 p.m.

★ REGULAR APPEARANCE OF LONDON ARTISTES ★

Membership 1/-   Admission 2/6

Enquiries : C. BENNETT · 112 NORTH LANE · ANGMERING-ON-SEA · SUSSEX

Initially Bob McDonald, Valerie Greenfield and myself were the residents. We were joined, shortly before Christmas, by Sarah Rhys from Brighton and then, on 21 January 1964 after a few appearances as a floor singer, by Jack Whyte a Scottish born teacher of English and drama who had moved to Brighton a few months earlier. Among the regular performers were Pauline Gowan and George Walker, mentioned in the Shoreham Herald report reprinted in Chapter five.

At the end of March 1964 I left to live and work in Folkestone, Kent and the running of the club was taken over by Bob McDonald.

After some seven months during which time the club continued to present star guests, including the inimitable Diz Disley, Bob also moved from the area and the club closed.

Pauline Gowan and George Walker
The author

Bob McDonald
The author

There have been further attempts at running clubs in the town but all have been short lived. First, early in 1971 there was a 'Blues and Contemporary' club meeting on Thursday evenings in The Lady Jane on Shoreham Beach. Resident at these meetings was Dick Wardell who, three years earlier, in the autumn of 1968, had been associated with the Blues Club at the Richmond in Brighton. Paul Holden remembers visiting the club and at the end of the evening joining singers and regulars when they adjourned to a nearby houseboat to continue with an informal session well into the night. By the summer of 1972 the meetings were monthly and the last mention of this club was by Jim Marshall in his weekly article in the Brighton and Hove Gazette in November of that year. In the mid 1980's the pub was renamed the Waterside Inn.

Next came a folk club at The Hebe organised by Pete Lunney, which ran for seven months in 1980 on alternate Thursday evenings from 22 May, when Uncle John's Band was featured as the guest, until 27 December. This hostelry, which was situated at the junction of Hebe Road and Victoria Road, was demolished in the late 1980's to make way for the development of a modern block of flats.

Eastbourne

The burgeoning Brighton 'folk revival' reached Eastbourne, its furthermost outpost, in 1963 when Johnie Winch and Rod Machling opened the *'Eastbourne Folk Club'* on Sunday evenings in The Railway [later renamed The Dolphin], South Street. At first they took turns, alternate weeks, to run the club since they were also running a club at the Stanford Arms, Brighton on the same evening and one of them had to be there.

Rod Machling and Johnie Winch *Jim Marshall*

Eventually Rod dropped out of the Eastbourne scene and Johnie continued on his own until handing the club on to John Peebles. In 1970 John prepared to close the club but in September Tony Cornish together with Ron Pope, Tom Groome and John Ticehurst offered to take over responsibility for running the sessions.

This was agreed and the club continued with Ron Pope as secretary and Tony Cornish as presenter and resident, although Johnie Winch did rejoin for a few months in 1971. Admission was 3/- [15 pence] for members and 4/- [20 pence] visitors. In December of that year however the organisers closed the club for a winter break, re-opening in the spring of 1972.

Tony Cornish
Tom Groome [courtesy of Ron Pope]

This club survived with varying degrees of success until October 1972 and during its life the guest list featured many local singers: Brian Golbey, Lea Nicholson, Keith Johns, Paul Setford, Terry Masterson, Don and Sarah Morgan, Vic and Tina Smith, Geoff Doel, Ivor Pickard, and Miles Wootton intermixed with the occasional national figure including Rosemary Harding, Roy Harris and Ian McCann.

Briefly in 1971 from 14 March to 20 June there was a folk session on Sunday evenings at The Habib coffee bar. Run by Audrey Judd, who also ran the Cuthbert Toad Hall club in Brighton, the residency was shared between Peter Collins and myself but only local singers were used in support. This was however to lead to the opening of Eastbourne's second folk club. As a result of singing at these sessions I made friends with people living in Eastbourne and sometimes visited them on Sunday evenings, during which we occasionally visited the folk club at the Dolphin. Early in 1973, finding that the club was closed and aware that people were interested in that type of music I decided, with encouragement from the landlord, to open the second *'Eastbourne Folk Club'*, again at The Dolphin, South Street. To avoid confusion with the previous club I opted to run the club on Thursday evenings with the opening night on Thursday 26 April 1973

The author at the opening night of Eastbourne [later Merrie England] Folk Club in The Dolphin.
The author

This was slow to develop but in the summer with the annual influx of foreign students keen to enjoy the British folk scene – then at the height of its popularity – there was a request from the landlord to organise a Sunday evening session and so, on Sunday 8 July 1973, the club started operating twice a week. On two occasions in August Keith Johns appeared as co-resident but at the beginning of September local teacher and melodeon player Ray Langton joined me as co-resident. These sessions, packed now not only with students but also many local enthusiasts, continued through the summer until September when the landlord moved on and the club was given notice. First the Sunday club closed on 9 September followed on the 13 by the Thursday club.

A new home was quickly found and the club transferred to The Crown, Crown Street, Old Town, Eastbourne where we renamed it *'The Merrie England Folk Club'* and it rapidly became a major Sussex folk venue with the clubroom frequently packed to capacity. Opening on Sunday 23 September 1973 it ran for eight years until July 1981 – although not without a few breaks.

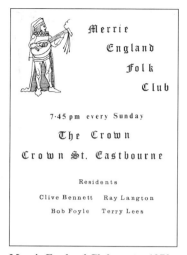

Merrie England Club poster 1973
The author

Ray Langton *The author*

At the height of its popularity this club brought major figures in the folk world to Eastbourne for the first time with Seamus Ennis [9 June 1974] Ewan MacColl and Peggy Seeger [11 October 1974] and The Watersons – including Martin Carthy – [16 October 1977] along with a veritable who's who of established singers including Alistair Anderson, Dave and Toni Arthur, Pete Bellamy, Alex Campbell, Bob Davenport, Etchingham Steam Band, John Foreman, Dave Goulder, Roy Harris, Nic Jones, John and Sue Kirkpatrick, Malcolm Price, Tony Rose, Martin Simpson, Isobel Sutherland, June Tabor, Eddie Upton and Martyn Wyndham Read.

The Sunday sessions continued until 20 November 1977 when they closed for the winter, reopening, still on Sundays, on 5 March 1978 These lasted until 3 September 1978 when they became monthly meetings, on the first Sunday of each month, until 1 April 1979 then weekly until 2 September when they reverted to monthly until 2 December. The club reopened for Easter 1980 from Sunday 30 March until 13 April and then again for the summer from 15 June to 24 August. By now there had been a change of landlord and in 1981 the club had to change to Friday evenings and ran only from 12 June until 31 July, almost exclusively for foreign students, when it finally closed.

In addition, during the summer of 1974, there was again a strong demand from foreign students for folk music and the club again operated on two evenings – Sundays and Thursdays. This was repeated for the next three years and the Thursday evening sessions were: 4 July to 29 August 1974, 19 June to 21 August 1975, 17 June to 12 August 1976 and 23 June to 18 August 1977. As with all folk clubs in the area at that time the annual influx of students was a welcome source of income but not without its problems. Club regular Ron Pope recalls, one Sunday evening at The Crown, Eastbourne there was the usual early mass of foreign visitors and on this particular occasion the front row was occupied by a group of Italian male students. They chatted away but as soon as one of the residents got up and started to sing the first song, to the amazement of singer and regular club members, they calmly took out a pack of cards and started dealing them out for a game. The song stopped in mid verse and it was explained to them in a few short words that whilst they were more than welcome to come to the club if they wanted to listen to the singing, if what they wanted to do was play cards, that would be better done downstairs in the bar.

Bob Foyle *The author*

Terry Lees c2000 *John Collyer*

When moving to The Crown Ray and I were joined as resident by Bob Foyle, a popular local singer/guitarist who regularly sang at The Pug 'O Junch club in Lewes, Terry Lees, acclaimed as one of the finest guitarist in the county and Allegra Carlton, although Allegra soon dropped out of the residency. Ray, together with his wife Bev were later to become established as the organisers of the Sidmouth Children's Festival while Terry Lees went on to achieve second place at the annual Guitarist of the Year competition at Wembley concert hall in 1998 before winning the competition two years later at Birmingham in 2000.

The most enduring 'regulars' at the club were Ron Pope, Tom Groome and John Ticehurst who had earlier been co organisers, along with Tony Cornish, of the first Eastbourne Folk Club and it was at The Crown that John Ticehurst – whose early death was mentioned in the 'Long Running Brighton Club' section – first sang in public.

Ron Pope, Tom Groome & John Ticehurst
Ron Pope

Inevitably over the eight years that the club ran the residents changed. First, Bob Foyle in late 1973 and then Ray Langton in May 1974, as work opportunities led them away from the area, to be replaced by Chris Fisher and then Dave Goodstone. Subsequent changes saw Don Bonito, Keith Duke – another teacher, Duncan Woods, Jim and Bernice Harding, Barry Walker and Lesley Smith – mentioned in the Brighton section where they were residents, Nick Westcott and John and Cindy Zarfass come and go as residents.

Duncan Wood *the author*

Of these, Duncan Wood was the most charismatic. Born in Scotland he was studying in Eastbourne and took up violin playing. Arriving at the folk club one Sunday evening he was given a floor spot, and gave an average performance. Next week he returned and was much improved and so on for several weeks by which time he was becoming not only very good but also extremely popular with the regulars. It then transpired he was teaching himself to play the fiddle and sitting in his flat all day, day after day, practising for eight to ten hours. He was soon invited to become a resident, which he accepted and settled into a regular slot. Then one week he arrived minus fiddle – "not playing this week?" he was asked. "Can't play any more" he replied to everyone's amazement. Then, in response to an enquiry as to "why not?" He explained that he had been to a concert at The Gardner Centre, Brighton to see Boys of the Lough and particularly his idol Aly Bain and from watching had realised he had taught himself an incorrect bowing technique. After some weeks he returned to the club with his fiddle having spent many, many more hours sitting in his flat un-learning his incorrect technique and teaching himself the correct one.

Several years later he married a Norwegian student working in Eastbourne and moved to Oslo. There he soon became a folk hero with several LP records and his own TV programme.

Returning to the opening of the Merrie England Club at The Crown in 1973, at Ray Langton's suggestion the residents agreed that if it was to be a member based club with an annual subscription – a standard format in folk clubs at that time - it should offer an opportunity for every member to take part in some kind of folk activity even if they could not or did not, wish to sing.

As a consequence an innovative approach led, during the winter months, to a series of folk workshops being organised on alternate Wednesday evenings with guitar classes led by Terry Lees, a sea shanty group led by Ray and myself and sword dancing and mumming led by Ray. Out of these sessions in 1974 came début performances from The Merrie England Mummers and Sword Dance team with four non singers – the group is still active today and is now, as

Associate Members of The Morris Ring and in their twenty seventh year, among the oldest revival Mummers Groups [Clubs] in the country, after Redcar and Coventry.

Sun 9 June 1974 Merrie England Sword Team at Eastbourne College Rag Week *Left to right:* **Colin Haverson, the author, Mike Anderson, Ray Marshall, Alastair Turner, A N Other and seated Ray Langton** *The author*

Sun 21 April 1974 Mummers first performance. The Crown, Eastbourne *Left to right:* **Mike Anderson, Ray Langton The author and Terry Lees** *The author*

Sun 14 April
1996
Merrie
England
Mummers at
Stratford
The author

Left to right: **Felix Byrne, Norman Hopson, Trevor Curry, the author, a guest holding MEM's Horse's skull, Eddie Scott, Mike Reilly and Ben Miller**

The success of this club spawned others in the mid 70's and first Tony Cornish opened a summer club, *'The New Contemporary Folk Society'*, specifically for foreign students, meeting at The Squirrel, Terminus Road on Tuesday evenings starting 23 April 1974 with the last published evening in June 1976. After this Terry Lees with Nick Westcott ran a session *'The Oval Folk Club'* on Tuesday evenings originally at The Oval then from 29 June to 3 August 1976 in The Mostyn Hotel, Wilmington Square. A little later, in November 1975, Kelvin Message – assisted by Dave Goodstone and later joined by Eric and Jane Downes, Bob Taylor and Gary Matthews – opened 'The Lamb Folk Club' on Wednesday evenings in The Lamb Inn, Church Street, which was to prove very popular until closing on 27 February 1980.

Kelvin Message *Tom Groome*
[courtesy of Ron Pope[

Next, Drew Knowles-Baker, assisted by Nigel French and, among others Kelvin Message, former residents of the Merrie England Club Chris Fisher and Dave Goodstone, Judy Hart and Paul Rawlinson, ran a Wednesday evening club in The Terminus, Terminus Road. This club opened on 3 February 1982 and closed on 17 December 1986 when it was discovered that the premises had no music licence. The guest list

87

featured many national figures including Bob Davenport and The Rakes, Martyn Wyndham-Read, Martin Carthy, Debby McClatchy, Peter Bellamy, Richard Digance and the Copper family. There was then a brief move to The Archery Tavern, Seaside Road but this only lasted from 27 March to 5 June 1987.

Chris Fisher *[below]* **and Dave Goodstone**
[right] Both Tom Groome [courtesy of Ron Pope]

On Wednesday 1 June 1988 a new sessions – *'The Star Folk Club'*, meeting fortnightly – started at The Star Inn, Star Road, Old Town organised by Kelvin Message and Chris Fisher. Early in 1990 this transferred round the corner to The Crown, Crown Street as *'Eastbourne Folk Club'*.

In 1997 the organising was taken over by Nick Westcott, former resident at the Merrie England Club, and Sean O'Rourke a long term regular at all the Eastbourne clubs. In January 1999 with serious competition from a loud jukebox and lack of sympathy from the landlord the club vacated the Crown and moved to the Lamb.

LEWES AND ISFIELD
The growing influence of the Brighton scene reached Lewes in 1965 when Jack Whyte, assisted again by Terry Masterson, opened the *'Pug O' Junch'* club at The Lewes Arms, Mount Place on Saturday evenings, commencing on 6 March of that year. This rather odd name came about because Jack, the club's founder, being an English teacher was, as Terry recalls, fond of spoonerisms and possibly too, by the notion that if one overindulged in alcoholic beverage one might inadvertently indulge in spoonerism.

Terry Masterson [guitar] and Jack Whyte [at Eastbourne Folk Club]
Tom Groome
[courtesy of Ron Pope]

When Jack left for Canada in July 1967 Terry continued to run the club bringing in Vic and Tina Smith in March 1970 as co residents until 1973 when he handed the club over to them. Admission, in 1970, was 3/- [15 pence] for members and 4/6 [22½ pence] visitors with an annual membership fee of 5/- [25 pence]. During this time, for a period of some

13 months, from 1 February 1971 to March 1972 Terry was away in the United States of America for an extended tour of club and college bookings. In May 1974 the club was renamed *'The Lewes Arms Folk Club'*.

Terry Masterson with Tina [Christine] and Vic Smith *Jim Marshall*

By 1975 Roddy Cowie had joined Vic and Tina as a resident and in January of the following year Terry rejoined along with Anne Loughran, followed soon afterwards by Dave Sykes and Paul Hawes.

On 9 August 1969 the club featured two Sussex traditional singers, George Belton and Bob Blake, and on 11 September 1971 Vic and Tina organised a Sussex Singers Night, an event that was to become a popular and regular feature of the Lewes folk club.

The 1971 session was a celebration of the eighty fifth birthday of Scan Tester, the Sussex concertina player and featured, apart from Scan, The Coppers from Peacehaven, George Belton from Madehurst and Bob Blake from Shipley.

George Belton at Lewes Folk Club
Tina and Vic Smith

George Spicer at Lewes
Tina and Vic Smith

Another popular feature was the club exchange nights, starting with Chichester and later the 'Fighting Cocks' from Kingston, Surrey then clubs in Horsham, Sevenoaks and Fishbourne.

Throughout this time the club achieved great popularity both with the Sussex based singers and folk enthusiasts, attracting near capacity audiences with its strong traditional bias and regular "Come All Ye" sessions rather than the constant use of star guests. When star guests were booked however they were always of the highest quality and included Seamus Ennis the magnificent Uillean piper and storyteller, acclaimed Sussex source singer George Spicer, folklorist supreme A L 'Bert' Lloyd, Alistair Anderson, Cyril Tawney, Martyn Wyndham-Read, Fred Jordan, Shirley and Dolly Collins, Peter Bellamy, John Kirkpatrick, Isabel Sutherland, Nic Jones, Roy Harris, Davy Graham, the Etchingham Steam Band, Sarah Grey, Ray Fisher, Queen of the Irish tinkers Margaret Barry, Frankie Armstrong, The McPeakes, Pecker Dunne, the irrepressible Reverend Kenneth Loveless, and the outstanding Scottish traditional performers Lizzie Higgins and Belle and Alec Stewart.

In 1970 a number of performers from the Brighton and Lewes clubs united to revive the Chithurst mummers' play, giving two performances for charity. This proved so popular that it was repeated in December 1971 and 1972 with performances at both The Pug O' Junch club in Lewes and the Sunday club at the Stanford Arms in Brighton.

Membership of the seven strong team varied but included Vic Smith, Terry Masterson and Paul Hawes from the Lewes club, Tim Broadbent, Jerry Jordan, Don Morgan, Eddie Upton, Roger Brasier, Chris Littledale and Keith Johns from both the Friday and Sunday folk clubs in Brighton and Bob Foyle who was a regular singer at Lewes and in 1974 became a founder member of the mummers group at the Merrie England Folk Club, Eastbourne.

Mumming at Lewes:
Left to right: **Terry Masterson, Jerry Jordan, Paul Hawes, Vic Smith and Chris Littledale**
Jim Marshall

Bob Foyle
Jim Marshall

Music was provided by Tina Smith who was also used as a 'stand in' for anyone unable to perform and on one particular occasion in 1971 at the Croydon Folk Club was a memorable 'Old Mother Christmas' in the absence of Bryan 'Father Christmas' Blanchard.

It was at the Lewes Arms also, on the 7 December 1974, Peter Pilbeam recorded the BBC's Radio Two weekly folk magazine 'Folkweave'. The club continued to flourish through the early and middle 1970's but by 1978 became unable to sustain big name bookings and after 26 August that year it changed to a weekly singaround. Then, with great reluctance, the club decided to break its thirteen years association with the Lewes Arms pub. This was due to several factors not least of which was a less than co-operative landlord together with the enforcement of more stringent fire precautions which resulted in a more claustrophobic atmosphere and a loss of some of the pub's character. In addition the club room, which was already small, but cosy, was suddenly reduced in size by the inclusion of a bar and permanent stage which almost halved the free space. As mentioned in an earlier chapter, the importance of the landlord is difficult to exaggerate. Tom and Joan Millard, mine hosts at the Lewes Arms at the time of the club's inception, were later to say to Jack and Terry "You boys have put us on the map!" This was a rare compliment from a pub landlord. Terry contrasted this with the attitude of the later landlord, at the time of the club's departure, which he summed up as "We don't need you."

So it was that from 11 October, the guest evening changed to a Wednesday at The Royal Oak, Station Street where the club had been organising folk dancing on the first Wednesday of each month, as reported by Jim Marshall in SOAPBOX in the Sussex Folk Diary number 52

"The folk scene is always changing and there are developments, too, within the Lewes club. The Lewes Arms, now no longer a financially viable venue for the big names, will, from September, run on Saturdays as a singers' club, whereas the Royal Oak in Station Street will become a weekly club meeting every Wednesday. The first Wednesday in each month will still be a dance night with the remaining Wednesdays devoted to song."

There was a strong line up of guests for the first month with Bob Davenport and The Rakes, Belle Stewart and Sheila MacGregor followed by Chris Foster but, as they say, the best laid plans! By November, problems with the licensing of the Royal Oak club room for safety during live performances, caused these sessions to become bar singarounds until February 1979. Vic Smith reported in the Mid Sussex Times on 7 November *"The Lewes folk club has been forced to cancel its very attractive autumn programme. The Royal Oak, where the club has been meeting, is scheduled for alterations including improvement of fire escape facilities. Until these are completed the authorities will not grant a music licence. The club is making do for the present by holding singaround evenings each Wednesday in the smaller downstairs clubroom."* He reiterated the problem in Sussex Folk Diary number 56:

"The loss of the excellent clubroom at the Royal Oak was a terrible blow to everyone involved in the Lewes Folk Club. All the dances that we had held there and the first few song evenings that we had managed had been very successful. We have not given up hope entirely of returning there but the alterations that would be needed to meet the requirements would be very expensive, despite the efforts being made by the management at the Royal Oak to find a workable scheme. With so many folk clubs feeling insecure in the tenure of their clubrooms it is ironic to have a pub like the Royal Oak where the landlady would really like to have a folk club but cannot. Lewes does not offer a vast range of suitable alternatives. There are a couple of possibilities for a club venue but not one that could see us starting immediately. However the club will start its activities again (rising like a phoenix from the ashes of fire regulations) because we have found an excellent venue for our monthly dances at the fairly new Bridge View Community Centre in Malling. We hope to be able to retain the informal atmosphere that pervaded at the Royal Oak dances and we invite other dance band musicians and callers to join the Lewes Band for the evening. There will also be opportunities for singers to get a hearing. This will be on the first Thursday of each month."

On 28 July 1979 – reverting to Saturday evenings – the club reopened at The Brewer's Arms, without Terry but with Isabel Sutherland, Bob Lewis, Will Duke and Vic and Sheila Gammon joining the residents. By then however there were many counter attractions on a Saturday evening and on 31 July 1980 the meetings changed to a Thursday evening.

As Vic Smith explained again, in Sussex Folk Diary number 64:

"The Lewes Folk Club has now been meeting at the Brewers Arms for a year and our stay there has been a happy and by and large successful one. However there have been some difficulties and so we have decided to make certain changes. The main problem has been that we met on Saturdays. Most of the resident singers also play in two folk dance bands, which frequently take them away from the club to play for Saturday dances. We ourselves have been to rather less than half the club meetings in the past year which we admit is a poor record for the main organisers. In addition, the club has had to compete with lots of popular Saturday dances, concerts and festivals that have clearly drawn away our regular supporters. So we have taken the decision to meet on Thursdays from July 31st. We will still have our monthly dances on the first Thursdays but these will be at the Brewers Arms. The other nights will be song nights with lots of leading groups and singers appearing. As well as those listed in our current programme in the next panel, we will be having Ossian and Ar Log in the autumn. Although "Come All Ye's" used to be some of our best evenings, they are no longer so successful, so we will be having more "Theme" evenings in which local performers can participate and also residents' invitation evenings when anything or everyone could be invited! Our first two theme evenings will be one on supernatural songs for Halloween and "Reynard The Fox" organised by Terry Masterson in November." Finally, we hope that a regular commitment on the part of the residents can bring back a continuity to the club and that our new format will prove popular both to participants and audience."

Despite these changes the club was on the move again on 4 February 1982 when it transferred out to The Laughing Fish, Isfield where Vic and Tina along with Vic Gammon and Terry Masterson continued as residents. Vic once more used the Sussex Folk Diary [number 73] to explain the move:

"From the beginning of February, Lewes Folk Club is going to move to the Laughing Fish at Isfield. This is just off the A26 road between Lewes and Uckfield. We will be leaving the Brewers Arms with some regrets as the landlord, Patrick Meagher has always been very fair to us, but we have to face the fact that the room is too large for our present purpose, and almost impossible to heat successfully in the winter. The Laughing Fish offers us a smaller, more intimate room which we feel has a great potential for folk music. The pub has already got associations with folk music, having been a popular Morris stand for many years as well as being the venue for lively sessions featuring the Biggest Trio in The World. The move will also be marked by a

change in policy. In future most nights will have free admission with a hat (or in this case the fish) coming round for collection. This money will be towards booking guests but there will also be feature nights, singarounds and club exchanges. In addition we will continue to book the top names in folk music, roughly once a month and there will be an admission charge with advance tickets available for these nights."

In the later days of The Lewes Arms folk club the evenings always started off with a few tunes, both to create a good club atmosphere and also because there were an increasing number of people learning instruments, who wanted somewhere to play. Barn dances were also becoming popular and bands were in demand. So, the Lewes Band was formed from regulars at the Lewes Arms club – Paul Hawes, Dave Sykes and Tina and Vic along with local tuba player Daphne Elston.

The Lewes Band.
[left to right]
Dave Sykes, Tina and Vic Smith, Paul Hawes and Daphne Elston.
Tina and Vic Smith.

The Lewes Band played a lot of venues in the Sussex area, for community and family events, but by the time The Laughing Fish club was going Paul had moved to Worcestershire and Dave had decided to leave so Tina and Vic teamed up with Brendan and Chrissie Buckley to form 'Four Piece Suite'. The band also did some songs and performed at various clubs in the area. Bren and Chrissie moved to Northumberland and a new band the Sussex Pistols gradually evolved from musicians in the area, including Tina and Vic with Bing Lyle [accordion], Ben Paley [fiddle], Dave Levett [bass] and Naomi Russel [fiddle and hammer dulcimer]. This band is still performing and much in demand today but along the way Tina and Vic found time to play with other song groups – a quartet 'Wattsmith' with Lyn [formerly O'Gorman] and Charlie Watts and 'The Celtic Fringe' with Terry Masterson, a name jokingly bestowed on them that somehow 'stuck'.

The latter group's first performances was at a Michelham Priory Folk Day just doing songs but later they started specialising in theme evenings such as Halloween.

After six years at the Laughing Fish, in August 1988, Tina and Vic handed the organisation over to Tony and Jane Graham who were joined in December that year as residents by Terry Lees. In June 1990 the club transferred to The

Royal Oak at Barcombe as *'Folk at The Oak'* and in September reduced the frequency of meetings to monthly on the first Thursday before closing on 6 December 1990. This club with a continuous record of over 25 years is the longest running club in the area.

Bing Lyle *Jim Marshall*

'Wattsmith'
[left to right]
Charlie and Lynn Watts,
Tina and Vic Smith
Tina and Vic Smith

Such a club dominates the folk scene in a small town; nevertheless there have been other clubs, many of which were organised by Fred Baxter. These include singaround sessions in the rear bar of The Black Horse, Western Road, initially on Sunday lunch times starting in November 1977, these proved so popular that in April 1978 they were extended to twice a week with another session every Tuesday evening. Both sessions continued until November 1981 when the landlord decided he needed the room to expand his catering facilities. After this they reverted to a single weekly session, held on Sunday lunch times in The Royal Oak, Station Street, again in the bar, finally closing in 1986 when the brewery decided to 'modernise' the pub and 'retire' Colette Chapman the popular landlady. All of these sessions were hosted by Fred Baxter, aided at various times by John and Cindy Zarfass, Tim Shave, Mike Jones, Ed and Pat Ford, Trevor Curry, Gordon Allen and myself.

Overlapping these informal singarounds Fred also founded a more formal club with *'Folk at The Elephant'* in The Elephant and Castle Hotel, White Hill which opened on Thursday 16 June 1977 featuring 'My Lorde Sheriff's Complainte' as the star attraction, and closed on 27 April 1978 with me as the final guest. Apart from Fred the club featured Jancis Gilbert and John Zarfass as co residents.

Fred Baxter
Tom Groome
[courtesy of Ron Pope]

Briefly, in October/November 1979, I organised a *'Lewes Singers Club'* meeting on Thursday evenings at The Royal Oak with Vic and Tina Smith, Sandra Goddard and Meic and Valmai Goodyear as 'regulars'.

Peter Dommen
Charlie Watts

Folk in the Oak poster 1982
The author

'FOLK IN THE OAK'

ROYAL OAK HOTEL
STATION STREET
LEWES

OPENING SUNDAY
8th AUGUST 1982
8 p.m.   -   10.30 p.m.

Opening Night 'Admission Free'
Thereafter :-
ADMISSION   70p.
FLOOR SINGERS   30p.

'COME YE ALL'

If you have never been to a Folk Club before then come to
this Opening Night and see what you have been missing.

After the Sunday lunch time singarounds mentioned earlier had transferred to the Royal Oak, Peter Dommen, one of the 'regular' drinkers at the pub and previously a visitor to Vic and Tina's club at the Brewers Arms which had then recently transferred to Isfield, fired with enthusiasm by the music and atmosphere of the sessions was lamenting the fact that Lewes no longer had a formal club with guest performers. "Why don't you start one, then!" was the response he received from Fred Baxter and with that Peter decided to open a formal club and invited Fred to act as co-host. This was *'Folk in The Oak'* and met on Sunday evenings in the upstairs clubroom of The Royal Oak. The club first met on 8 August 1982 with Wilbury Jam as the guests and Fred Baxter, Gordon Allen, Tim Shave, myself and the group 'Athol Brose' – comprising Ivor George, Keith Burton and Lyn O'Gorman, as residents.

After four months Gordon Allen was replaced by Ray 'Pikey' Whiteway-Roberts and in April 1983 Ivor George and Lyn O'Gorman became involved in the organisation until it closed in March 1985 – during this period the residents included Trevor Curry, Bob Rose, Ian Fyvie, Terry O'Connor and Pat Ford.

The Royal Oak was then refurbished and the club was forced to seek a new venue, moving to Monday evenings in The Ship Bar of the Brewers Arms where, by then, Peter was head barman. The club featured a mixture of local and national guests including Peta Webb and Pete Cooper, Martin Simpson and Vic Gammon but before long the club ran into problems similar to those encountered by Terry Masterson at the Royal Oak in Brighton in as much as the landlord wanted to invest money in 'big name' guests but was then annoyed when the result often was a huge loss. This led to Peter giving up and the club closed. The last advertised date was 28 July 1986 although there was a brief attempt to re-establish the sessions in the autumn with an informal sing-around on the first and third Wednesdays.

Next came a blend of dance and song at The Brewer's Arms in the High Street. Commencing 3 September 1986, there was a singaround on the first and third Wednesday of the month, a Ceilidh on the second Wednesday hosted by Maxwell's Demon, another Ceilidh on the fourth Wednesday hosted by Rosbif and a Singers Night with a booked guest on the occasions that there was a fifth Wednesday in the month. These sessions closed after a few months, the singarounds in January and the Ceilidhs in March 1987

Trevor Curry *George Wagstaff*

Lewes was not however exclusively a traditional music centre. On 6 August 1968 a *'Blues Club'* was opened on Tuesday evenings at the Lewes Arms but stayed there for only five weeks before moving to larger premises at the Richmond in Brighton. These sessions were hosted initially by Roger Hubbard, Nigel Manzel and Dick Wardell's Blues Band but at the end of the month they were augmented by the addition of Sam Mitchell.

More recently – from 5 December 1987 – Fred Baxter restarted a Saturday evening club in The Lewes Arms, Mount Place – the *'Lewes Arms Folk Club'*, which is still running. In so doing he hoped to re-establish the old Saturday evening connection and accordingly invited Terry Masterson, as one of the original residents, to join him in the venture. Following careful consideration Terry declined as he felt it would not be possible to recapture the club's former atmosphere. Initially the residents, along with Fred, were Tony and Jane Graham who, as mentioned earlier, subsequently took over running the club at The Laughing Fish, Isfield. After the first year the group was expanded, as the Folk Diary reported in Issue 114 for December 1988: *"Sandra Goddard has joined the team of residents at the Saturday club at the Lewes Arms in Lewes."* Later, after Tony Graham left the club, George Wagstaff a non singer, who had been involved with Friday's Folk in Brighton joined Fred and became responsible for organising the club with Fred as the compère.

George then left in 1991 and the organisation was taken over by a committee consisting of a group of residents, which included Fred. Then, as his health started to fail, Fred eventually gave up his position as a resident, retiring to live in Peacehaven then Seaford and finally Exeter where he died in 1998. Today, in the first year of the new millennium, the club is still run by a group of long term residents comprising Sandra Goddard, Valmai Goodyear, George Oakley and David Middleton supported by their newer regulars, Roger Brasier, who has recently returned to live in Brighton, Roy Nash from the Steyning singaround club, Dave Earl who is also a resident at The Wellington in Seaford and Derek Seed from Eastbourne.

One night in the spring of 1990 Terry Masterson and his wife Carole visited the Elephant and Castle to listen to Tim Kent and Ivor George who were doing a 'gig' in the bar. During the course of the evening Terry noticed the back room which was probably reserved for functions and was intrigued to find the walls decorated with guitars and other paraphernalia and thought what a wonderful venue for a folk music club.

The idea would probably have lain dormant but at the end of the evening, as he and his wife, having said their 'good-byes', were on their way home they were called back by Tim. He had apparently been singing Terry's praises to the landlord who wanted to offer Terry a 'gig' in the bar. Having had past experience of pub singing he was not over excited at this type of exposure but agreed to accept if he could use the back room and run it in his own way. This meant he would do three long spots during the course of the evening and invite guest performers to supply the bits in between. The landlord agreed and so, on 23 May 1990, Folk at the Elephant re-appeared as weekly sessions every Wednesday and soon proved enormously popular, lasting right through the summer. They would probably have survived much longer had it not been for the football season. One Wednesday meeting happened to clash with a big match on television and Terry waited most of the evening for the fans to leave so that he could start his session, finally giving up in disgust and going home, feeling that the landlord could have warned him and cancelled the music for the evening. The landlord never contacted him and he never went back.

Tim Kent and Ivor George
Tim Kent

In October, following the closure of Noble Folk in Brighton and with Paul Metsers as the first guest the sessions were taken over by Tim Kent and continued until February 1993. To pay for the guests Tim introduced the system of 'fines', which had been so successful at Nobles Folk in Brighton.

This was soon followed on 15 April 1993 by the town's latest club *'Folk at the Royal Oak'* at The Royal Oak, Station Street, Lewes organised jointly by Jim Marshall and Vic and Tina Smith – further links with the Brighton scene.

Jim, as ever, was ensconced by the door – but inside the room – collecting the entrance money, with Vic and Tina and two masterly musicians, Dan Quinn and Will Duke, holding the evening together as the residents. In July 1995 however Jim stepped down leaving the running of the club entirely with Vic and Tina and George Wagstaff tending the door.

Vic and Tina Smith
Jim Marshall

At the Royal Oak, as with all their previous clubs, Vic, Tina and Jim soon boasted an impressive list of guest singers including Martyn Wyndham-Read, Bob Davenport, The Rakes, Martin Carthy and Dave Swarbrick, Sara Grey, John Kirkpatrick, Dick Gaughan, Debbie McClatchy, Barry Dransfield, Fred Jordan, Ray Fisher, Jake Thackray, Cathal McConnell, Oliver Bootle and Ben Dauncey, Michael Marra, Vic Legg, Makvirag from Budapest, Alistair Anderson and Will Atkinson, John Foreman, Martin and Eliza Carthy with Norma Waterson and Sheila Stewart –

daughter of Belle Stewart of Blairgowrie. There were return visits to Sussex of past Brighton residents with Allan Taylor, Pete Stanley and Brian Golbey and Vic Gammon. A regular feature was an evening to celebrate Bob Copper's birthday and Vic reintroduced the Sussex Singers Night featuring Shirley Collins as host with the Copper family, Louie Fuller, Gordon Hall, Ron Spicer and Bob Lewis.

Will Duke and Dan Quinn
Jim Marshall

SEAFORD

Seaford, initially, differed from most of the other towns in the Brighton area in as much as it developed, albeit not until 1976, its own folk revival clubs. However none of the early clubs were very long lived and it was not until 1992, some thirty years after the song revival first reached the coast that a longer running club emerged. This later club is another that falls into the category of those influenced by the early Brighton scene. It opened at The Wellington, Steyne Road, Seaford with the first meeting on 7 February 1992 featuring the popular Sussex traditional singer Ron Spicer as the guest. *'The Wellington Folk Club'* operated with George Wagstaff as a non singing organiser and myself as compère – George, together with Eddie Upton, had been organisers in its latter days of the old Friday's Folk Club at The Springfield in Brighton and I had been involved with the first Ballads and Blues club.

George Wagstaff *Jim Marshall*

The choice of the venue was chance and the idea of opening a club was instinctive for two-experienced club organisers. On 15 December 1991 the Merrie England Mummers, who included George and myself, were on a Sunday lunchtime tour and finished early at the Royal Oak in Lewes. With time for another performance it was suggested that the group go down to Seaford where Barry Dimmack the former landlord of The Laughing Fish at Isfield had taken over the Wellington. On arriving at the pub both George and I took one look at the clubroom, opposite the bar, and decided it was ideal for a folk club. After performing our play and before leaving we had agreed on the organisation, the opening date and booked the room.

The author at Seaford Oct 2000
The author

For the first year I was the sole resident but early in 1993 I was joined by Dave Garner who although he lived in Seaford had been associated with The Hangleton Manor Folk Club in Hove.

In 1994 when Dave left the area Mary Barr took his place as resident. Early in 1995 George decided to retire from the club and the organising was taken over by a group of regulars who, without becoming a formal committee, volunteered to 'manage' key areas of the administration of the club. This consisted of Eileen Baldock as Treasurer her husband Ian handling Public relations, Mary Barr carrying out publicity and myself booking guest artistes while continuing as compère.

The following year the addition of Hazel Rose and a family group 'Rigmarole' comprising Ann Galvin with son Rob and daughter Kathryn extended the resident base.

Apart from the residents the Sussex traditional singer and musician Ron Spicer was an almost permanent feature of these sessions from 1992 until shortly before his death in 1996. In 1997, when Rob Galvin moved on to University, Rigmarole dropped out of the residency and their place was taken by Dave Earl. Two years later in 1999 the resident base was extended again by the addition of Grace Morrison, a Scot who had moved to Seaford a few months earlier, then the following year Hazel decided to stand down as a resident although continuing to appear from time to time as a floor singer. More recently Steve Nevill, a musician with the Long Man Morris side from Eastbourne has joined the residents.

Although the club had started with a policy of presenting mainly local singers, as it became more established this expanded to cover countrywide performers and major national figures including John Foreman, Roy Harris, Frankie Armstrong, Hughie Jones – formerly of The Spinners, Martyn

Wyndham-Read, Jeremy Taylor, Dave Webber and Annie Fentiman, Tim Laycock and the New Scorpion Band, Dave Goulder, and Louis Killen alongside traditional singers Fred Jordan from Shropshire, Mike Tickell from Northumberland and Sussex based Gordon Hall, Clare Clayton, Ken Spicer and the Coppers from Peacehaven.

Mary Barr
The author

Dave Earl
The author

Hazel Rose   **Steve Nevill**   **Grace Morrison**
The author   *The author*   *The author*

As already mentioned this is not however the first folk club in the town although none of the previous ones could be said to have had a direct link with the early Brighton folk revival.

The first club in Seaford was much earlier, in 1969/70, in the semi basement bar of the Bay Hotel on The Esplanade run by Ben Dallimore. Later, on Thursday evenings, in May 1976 there was another club, organised by Ray Hately and Mark Orchin at The Old Plough on a fortnightly basis with Glympstone Ryble and Ben Dallimore as residents. Early guests included Derek Brimstone, John Copper, Terry Lees and The Taverners. Then, from 1 July, the club moved to regular weekly meetings at The Sea Hotel with the residents expanded to include Keith Duke, Liz and Ian Hempstead and, briefly, Duncan Wood.

After this club closed there was a break until January 1978 when a new club opened on Sunday evenings at The Great Dane. This club, organised initially by Ian and Liz Hempstead and in its later life by Chris Sturdy, Corrine Darling and Martin Angel, survived for twelve months. It presented a range of local singers as guests and a variety of residents including, in addition to the organisers, Ray Hately, Chris Sturdy, Don Kelly, Bob Denmark, Mark Gunstone and myself. In November the club booked one of its few outside guests with an appearance by Alistair Anderson but in December it closed.

Almost at once it was replaced by the *'Seven Sisters Folk Club'* meeting on Friday evenings in the pub of that name. The club was organised by Christine Gray and opened on 5 January 1979 with Wilbury Jam as the first guests. In November, with support on the wane it dropped to fortnightly meetings but still managed to host Cilla Fisher and Artie Trezise on 30 November before closing on 21 December with a Christmas party which included Christine Hase and the Merrie England Mummers. Dave Fisher was the main resident throughout its life and others included, at various times, Liz and Ian Hempstead, Mark Gunstone, Martin Angel, Gordon Allen, Ed Ford and Trevor Curry.

Moving on in time to 1992 there was briefly *'The Concert Club'* organised by Don Partridge, again at The Seven Sisters which ran on Thursdays evenings on a monthly basis from the winter of 1992 to May 1993 and featured a range of contemporary and blues singers and guitarists including Bert Jansch and Cliff Aungier.

MILTON STREET

A few miles inland from Seaford, from 5 October 1978 until 9 August 1979, Martin and Sue Angel organised folk singing at *'The Ox Folk Club'* meeting at The Sussex Ox, Milton Street on Thursday evenings. Their co-resident throughout was Fred Baxter from Lewes and in June 1979 they were joined by Ed Ford. Apart from featuring many local singers as guests during its short life the club also presented Isabel Sutherland on 7 December 1978, Ian Anderson on 22 March and Shirley and Dolly Collins on 19 April 1979 While Vic Smith noted in the Mid Sussex Times on 16 March 1979 *"The Ox Folk Club, which meets at the Sussex Ox in Milton Street, just outside Alfriston, has its biggest night so far next Thursday evening when they have Alistair Anderson as guest. The club was started by Martin Angel and Fred Baxter last October and they realised that their first problem was going to be attracting enough people to their very rural venue during the winter months. Well, they have survived their first hurdle. Running a programme that was based exclusively on local singers, they have seen themselves through this bleak winter and now they are arranging a more adventurous programme for the spring and summer."* Unfortunately the rural location and a desire by the landlord to develop the catering facilities of the establishment led to the club closing four months later.

PEACEHAVEN

Peacehaven, like Seaford, is another town where interest in folk song developed outside the influence of Brighton. This perhaps is hardly surprising when many would argue that the area is one of the cradles of traditional singing in Sussex and particularly the harmony style made famous by the Copper family. As early as 1963 I remember driving over from East Preston in West Sussex to Woodingdean to collect Bob McDonald and then on to Rottingdean to pick up Ron Copper from the Queen Victoria. From there we made our way to Peacehaven to spend an informal evening in the Central Club, reminiscing and singing around the bar with Ron and Bob Copper. The first time this happened it was a Monday evening, Bob Copper was behind the bar and the four of us were the only people in the club during the whole evening.

Some years later Bob started an occasional folk night at the club and Vic Smith, writing in the Brighton Folk Diary for November/December 1971 reminisces on his early experience of these sessions. *"The first time that I went to the Central Club at Peacehaven was for a folk night in November 1969 Amongst the singers there were the Young Tradition, Tim Hart and Maddy Prior, Shirley Collins, Lea Nicholson, Trevor Crozier, Martyn Wyndham-Read, Allan Taylor and a host of other top names on the folk scene. It would have cost hundreds of pounds to put these artists on in a concert or a club, but on this occasion they were appearing free; in fact they had come mainly to listen rather than to sing because the licensee at the Central Club is Bob Copper, and this was one of the very special and very occasional "Copper Evenings".*

Bob and Ron Copper in the Central Club
Bob Copper

Later still, on 4 November 1971, when Bob Copper was becoming possibly even better known through his books on Sussex country life and folk songs, the family organised their own folk club *'Copper Song Folk'*. Meeting on the first Thursday of each month at The Central Club, South Coast Road, Peacehaven with the Copper family as 'mine hosts' – Bob and Ron having been joined by Bob's son John and daughter Jill. They were at first supplemented as residents by Vic and Tina Smith but by May 1978 Eric Meadows and Stuart Reed shared the support.

The club was a great favourite as Vic Smith reported in the Mid Sussex Times on 27 May 1976 *"The best known family for traditional singers in Sussex is undoubtedly the Copper family of Rottingdean. Bob Copper was the licensee of the Central Club in Peacehaven and there he started a monthly folk club five years ago. His son John is now the landlord there and their folk club is undoubtedly the best attended of all our local clubs. John and Bob and other members of the family still offer the club members their famous harmony singing every month, and next Thursday they will appropriately enough have another two Sussex traditional singers as their guests. They are Cyril Phillips from Borde Hill, and George Spicer from West Hoathly."*

As befitted such a renowned traditional family many of their guests were personal friends and equally revered in the folk world. Within the first eighteen months they included Seamus Ennis for the opening night, Shirley Collins, George Belton, Scan Tester, Isabel Sutherland, Bob Roberts, Belle and Alex Stewart, Fred Jordan and Peter Bellamy. This immensely popular monthly session continued until January 1987 and was unusual in that it was one of only two clubs nationally with not just individuals but several generations of a family of traditional singers as residents [the other being the Elliots of Birtley, Co. Durham]. Seven years later on 23 August 1994 the Coppers staged a 'one off' special evening of traditional songs and tunes at the Central Club featuring the American singer and multi instrumentalist Jeff Warner.

In between there was a regular Monday evening folk session at The Dewdrop Inn which ran for eight years from January 1976 to September 1984. Organised by Brian and Margaret Dowdall until August 1983 when the booking of guests and financial control was taken over by Don Murren although Brian and Margaret continued as residents. Briefly, from 6 Jan 1984 until the summer, the meetings changed to Friday evening. Initially the residents at this *'Monday Club'* were Brian Dowdall and John Zarfass [also known as John Basset], formerly partner of Indrani Shough, but in the autumn of 1976 Margaret joined her husband and later both Jo Gurr and Chris Sturdy featured as co-residents. The club, although relatively small, encouraged all forms of folk culture including poetry and whilst established performers were booked from time to time the club policy was to promote local singers rather than booking expensive 'named' artistes and through this approach a number of local performers received their first 'guest' booking.

Brian and Margaret Dowdall
Jim Marshall

Brian and Margaret opened a second club meeting on Friday evenings at the Gay Highlander on 6 January 1978 with John Lake and Dave Langridge "Lake and Ridge" as residents and The Taverners as the first guest but this proved to be a short-lived venture. "Lake and Ridge" performed a repertoire of mainly contemporary songs in a country music style, much of which was composed by Dave Langridge.

In the summer of 1984 the club which had been meeting on Friday evenings at the Dewdrop reverted to Mondays and changed name to the *'Oasis Club'* with a broad based folk and country style and Brian and Margaret as residents, but this closed in October 1984.

ROTTINGDEAN

In the traditional home of the Copper family however a folk song club was less successful. *'Rottingdean Folk Club'* organised by non singing Roger Corsons opened on 4 January 1978, initially at The Olde Place Club. Meetings were on Wednesday evenings and featured all the usual top local performers as guests: Alan White for the opening night followed by John Collyer, Pam Fereday, Lake and Ridge, Vic and Tina Smith, Miles Wootton and Don Kelly. In May 1978 it transferred to the White Horse Hotel on the seafront but closed soon afterwards.

FIRLE

The influence of the Brighton scene was not confined to towns; local villages were also developed as folk centres. The Ram at Firle has become possibly the most popular venue in the county for informal folk related sessions.

In 1974 a group of local musicians formed the Pump and Pluck band to perform traditional music from the south of England. The name was derived from characteristic instruments the band used, concertinas, melodeons and banjo.

The following year they were booked to tour Switzerland and as a result two of the highly talented musicians, Vic Gammon and Will Duke, decided the group should hold an unadvertised dress rehearsal for which they chose The Ram as an appropriate venue. This was on the first Monday of the month and became a regular, but still unadvertised, event devoted mainly to tunes with just a few songs.

Pump and Pluck Band
[left to right]
John Magill, Ian Holder, Vic Gammon, Sheila Magill [later Sheila Gammon], Jenn Price, Will Duke and Ed Bassford [caller]
Will Duke

After about a year the landlord asked them to change the night as the first Monday coincided on several occasions with Bank Holidays and the session moved to the second Monday of each month. These gatherings, in the main bar, continue until the present day, now under the guidance of Will since Vic moved away from the area in 1991, firstly to West Sussex and then to Leeds where he teaches music in the Education Department of Leeds University. These are not however the only folk sessions in this pub.

Will Duke *Will Duke*

A regular event known as *'Sussex Singers Night'* is held on the second Tuesday of each month in the back bar under the guidance of John Copper and Bob Lewis. Once again these are not advertised to the general public but are a meeting of traditional performers and invited friends sharing a love of folk song and providing the opportunity to learn not only songs but also more about the whole culture of folk traditions from source singers. The evening is not however solely dedicated to music and song but is a social gathering and includes refreshments.

They originated around 1971/72 as a social occasion for traditional performers from around the county who otherwise only met at clubs and festivals. The idea grew from George Belton, John Copper and Bob Lewis along with George Spicer and Cyril Phillips. Originally they met at pubs in the east, centre and west of the county; The George and Dragon at Dragon Green, The Fox at Charlton and the backroom of the Central Club in Peacehaven. Over the years the venues changed several times and included notably the Norfolk at Steyning, the Fountain at Ashurst and the White Horse in Sutton. Around 1990/1 however they settled at The Ram where they continue to the present day.

In 1988 Sandra Goddard handed over the monthly sessions at the Thatched Inn, Keymer, mentioned later, to John Townsend. Within weeks she opened a new song session, this time at The Ram. From then until the present day the pub has been the venue for these regular sessions held in the back bar on the third Tuesday each month. These informal gatherings were and still are advertised solely by word of mouth.

Not one of these three organised sessions is a 'folk club' in the formal sense. Each of the organisers would repudiate that label seeing their session as a meeting of friends and people with a common interest. They are however an integral part of the Brighton folk scene at the end of the twentieth century.

DITCHLING

In 1978 Brighton Morris dancer and singer Brian Ablett together with Sandra Goddard started a singaround session in the Cottage Bar of the North Star, Ditchling, and these became regular *'Folk Nights'* from Monday 4 September 1978 This was recorded by Vic Smith when he reported in the Mid Sussex Times on 31 August of that year *"Mid Sussex is to have a new folk club to meet at the North Star, Ditchling. At the moment this is to take the form of an informal sing-a-round and music session in the bar. A trial evening run by the organiser, Brian Ablett, turned out to be a great success and now Brian has arranged for the session to take place on the first Monday of each month, first one being next Monday. Brian is keen to get as many singers and musicians as possible along to get things off to a good start."* The following year, on 19 February they were moved to the third Monday of the month. The last advertised date for these meetings was 15 December 1980 when commercial development of the pub made it more difficult to sing in the bar.

In 1998 however the sessions were resurrected and the Folk Diary No.175 for February/March 1999 carried an advertisement *"We've taken off! After a successful start in '98 Ditchling Folk Nights are on the map. At the Sandrock [High Street] Ditchling on the last Monday of the month."*

KEYMER

The North Star sessions were not however the only free folk evenings in the area just north of the Downs. At various times over many years both Friday's Folk and The Sunday Club in Brighton enjoyed the hospitality of Jim and Heather Keelty at The Springfield. When they left in July 1980 Jim Marshall in

The Sussex Folk Diary No.52 SOAPBOX commented on the critical influence a landlord had on the success or failure of a folk club and how much such a good landlord would be missed.

"A landlord, as most organisers will confirm, can easily make or break a folk club. We've all heard the tales of club rooms being turned into discos, games rooms, restaurants and the like and there's very little that a club can do in such circumstances. After all, the landlord is the boss and he doesn't run his pub solely for the folk fraternity.

This being the case makes it even more difficult when a good landlord decides to move.

Heather and Jim, mine hosts at the Springfield Hotel in Brighton, are leaving at the end of July and to say that they'll be missed is a great understatement. They've been good friends to both the Friday and Sunday clubs-sympathising with us on the bad nights and sharing our excitement on the good ones. We're going to miss them and their cries of "Come along now boys and girls", but we wish them great success at their new pub, the Thatched Inn in Keymer."

Heather Keelty and Laurie Goddard
Terry Masterson

It was perhaps not altogether surprising therefore when on 21 April 1981, at Heather and Jim's invitation, Brian Ablett and Sandra Goddard, co-organisers at the Ditchling Folk Night sessions, opened another singaround club just a few miles from Ditchling, meeting on the third Tuesday each month at their new hostelry, The Thatched Inn, Keymer.

Although pressure of work led to Brian withdrawing from organising in 1983 Sandra maintained the sessions until 1988 when John Townsend assumed the mantle of co-ordinator until they ended in May 1992.

In 1988 Jim and Heather left Keymer to return to the Springfield in Brighton but the new landlord of the Thatched Inn was the ideal host for a folk club as the Folk Diary recorded in Issue 111 for June of that year: *"The new landlord of the Thatch is an ex-member of the Martlet Morris Men and a supporter of the Chichester folk club in the days when it met at the Hole In The Wall."*

These sessions proved very popular and regularly attracted a horde of talented local singers and musicians, making the need of guest performers superfluous. Singers arrived not just from the Brighton area but also further afield towns such as Haywards Heath, Crawley, Horsham and even south London.

STEYNING

More recently a highly acclaimed singaround club opened in 1993 meeting on the first and third Mondays of each month in the Norfolk Arms, Church Street, Steyning. Hosted by Roy Nash, mentioned earlier as a regular performer at the first Hastings folk club, and Noel Dumbrell, a local singer from a traditional background, they were supported by a host of popular Sussex singers including Harry Mousdell, formerly of Horsham, Jerry Jordan, and Sandra Goddard from Lewes and Dave Earl from Hove all three of whom have had long associations with the Brighton folk scene.

Noel Dumbrell and Roy Nash
The author

Paul Holden *[above] and* **Harry Mousdell** *[right]* **at the Norfolk Arms, Steyning. May 2001** *The author*

110

FOOTNOTE

Before leaving the folk clubs it is interesting to look at two aspects of the scene, firstly the singers from a singers view point and secondly the pub landlords from an organisers perspective.

Miles Wootton, writing in the Sussex Folk Diary No.48 in November 1977 as the folk boom started to fade said:

"I am a folk club fan. I love them all – even the bad ones. And as a leisure-time singer and writer I owe the clubs a lot. Where else could I find a sympathetic audience with such a congenial atmosphere, and sometimes even get paid for pursuing my hobby?

Herein lies the uniqueness of the system. It provides a perfect outlet for various and varying talents, spanning a wide range of entertainment. Let no one tell you that folk-clubs are mainly about folk music, despite the traditional bias of many excellent ones. They are more a kind of cottage industry for producing and encouraging home-grown amateur talent.

But what of the professionals? Well, if by that you mean people who get their living from the clubs, there are plenty of them. But, judged impartially, and winkled out of the cosy folk-club womb where they are known and loved, some would present a strange picture to the real world outside.

You have met them; the over dedicated Traddie, fanatically hunting for [deservedly] obscure versions of obscure, often meaningless songs; the "Serious" Contemporary Singer-Songwriter, whose banal lyrics are somehow highlighted by his invariably immaculate guitar work; the Very Jokester who takes a pride in never actually getting around to singing the song he so laboriously introduces; the "Country" musician from the Kingston Bypass, dressed like a Mississippi gambler, sawing or picking with all the enthusiasm of an alcoholic for a mug of cocoa.

We should face the fact that, taking the population as a whole, "Folk" music has about as much appeal to the average Englishman as Backgammon does to the Masai warriors. Folk-clubs exist for the interested minority and they are all the better for that. They are not commercial propositions, and were never intended to provide a living for people who, with rare exceptions, would be singing elsewhere if they had more general appeal."

As mentioned elsewhere the pub landlord could make or break a club. John Towner, long time organiser of the Black Horse club at Telham, near Hastings wrote on the subject in the Sussex Folk Diary No.39 "Soapbox" in May 1996:

"This little missive is aimed, not only at all of you folk club-going fanatics but also at any folk artists that might happen to glance at this page. I would like to put the folk club organisers problems into perspective.

You will all, no doubt, have seen Robin Dransfield's little moan about club organisers, about a year ago, and the pros and cons that developed from it. However all the letters that flew to and fro in Melody Maker and Folk Review failed to pinpoint the all-powerful force behind each folk club. I give you friends – "THE LANDLORD".

Jim Marshall and I have suffered many setbacks imposed by our genial hosts, who have sometimes required exorbitant amounts for the rental of their "attractive" rooms. I, personally, have encountered a landlord who interrupted Martyn Wyndham-Read in order to say that a car was badly parked, switched off the lights to plunge Etchingham Steam Band into the dark and cut off John and Sue Kirkpatrick rudely, in full song, to clear the club with still ten minutes drinking-up time in hand [The last named was enough for me by the way – I left].

Even as I write this article, news has reached me that a well known Sussex folk club has had to close down due to interference by the landlord and his family, who had the temerity to insult Louis and Sally Killen [the mind boggles].

I think my favourite happening, though, was at an ill-fated club that I ran in Bexhill which used to struggle along every week attracting about twenty-five people. I arrived one Saturday night to find that the landlady had installed an electric guitar and fiddle player in a downstairs room, and was covering the front of the pub with posters, advertising them as "admission free".

I am now, however, happily ensconced at the Black Horse, Telham where the landlord, Eddie, has been connected with the folk club for nine years. He understands my problems and I understand his. Together, in my opinion, we run one of the happiest folk clubs in England and long may it be so."

5   THE MEDIA
LOCAL RADIO, THE PRESS AND PUBLICITY

With so much interest in folk music over the past forty years it is interesting to reflect on how this was covered by the local media and how the clubs publicised their events.

The Press
When Terry Scarlett and I opened the first Brighton Ballads and Blues Club in the autumn of 1961 we spent many hours of the preceding weekends walking round the town trying to persuade shopkeepers to display small posters advertising the sessions. In addition we contacted the local papers and by the use of TV stars Robin Hall and Jimmie MacGregor as opening night guests, secured good coverage both before and after the event. This approach we successfully repeated a few weeks later for the Pete Seeger one man concert in Hove. In general however the local press showed little interest in folk music and the club relied for publicity on handbills and brief newsletters, which were distributed at club meetings or posted to club members.

This format was repeated when we opened a club in Worthing for the summer of 1962 but again, apart from good coverage for the opening night, the local press showed little interest.

In the autumn of 1963 however I received rather more assistance from the Shoreham Herald when I opened a club at the Burrell Arms near the town's railway station. The local paper not only covered the opening but was willing to print a brief report weekly on the previous week's session if it had 'local' interest in the form of names of people involved.

I provided regular copy and typical of the reports published was the one in the paper dated Friday 21 February 1964 under the heading *"Leading 'Blue Grass' group"* which said *"More than 50 people were at Shoreham Folk Song Club in the Burrell Arms on Tuesday to hear England's leading 'Blue Grass' group, The Hickory Nuts, who made their first record last week.*
Paul Plum, of Shoreham was there with his recording equipment.
Other performers during the evening were the residents, Clive Bennett, Bob McDonald and Jack White [Whyte], *and local members Pauline Gowan, of Shoreham, George Walker, of Lancing, Paul Setford and Geoff Biddle, both of Worthing, and Jim Hoare, of Shoreham with his fiddle."*

While the folk boom rapidly developed during the mid 60's the local press, in general, gave folk clubs little or no coverage.

From December 1966 through to the end of 1967 Jim Marshall produced a series of monthly 'Newsletters' for the Stanford club. At the same time, concerned at the lack of publicity the clubs were receiving – particularly from the local press, he wrote to the editor of The Brighton and Hove Gazette suggesting they should add a folk column alongside their existing Jazz section.

The reply said simply they had no one able to do it but if he cared to take the job on – informally and unpaid of course – they would consider including it. So it was that Jim became an honorary newspaper journalist with a weekly column that was to run for some 14 years, providing local folk enthusiasts with an invaluable and comprehensive folk 'What's On', illustrated with data on guest singers and news from the folk scene.

There was a distinct move from reporting what had happened to informing readers of forthcoming events.

The first article appeared on 16 June 1967 *[reproduced below]* but future articles were all illustrated with a picture, usually one of the guest singers at a local club during the following weekend but from time to time featuring a local club resident.

"THE FOLK SCENE

By Jim Marshall
Although the summer is traditionally a quiet time as far as folk clubs go, there appears to be no let-up on the Brighton scene.
For instance tonight at the Springfield Hotel, Springfield Road, Friday's Folk have as their guest Isabel Sutherland, perhaps Scotland's finest singer of traditional songs.
Miss Sutherland, who comes from Edinburgh, first heard Scots folk song from her grandmother, sister of a well-known piper of his day, Andrew Waters of Penicuik. She has recorded for many different companies, her most recent album being a fine selection on Topic called "Vagrant Songs of Scotland."
Completing the entertainment are the club's two resident singers Jack Whyte and Terry Masterson plus any number of local singers who are always likely to drop in.
If your interest lies more towards the American style of pickin' and singin', you'll be interested to hear that Tom Paley is the special guest at the Stanford Arms Folk Club, Preston Circus, Sunday.
Tom was a founder member, together with Mike Seeger and John Cohen, of the New Lost City Ramblers. On leaving the Ramblers he formed a new group, the Old Reliable String Band, with which he recorded an excellent album on the American Folkways label.
He then came over to London where he lectures in mathematics part of the time and sings the rest. He filled the Stanford to overflowing when he was there some three years ago. The residents at this club are Rod Machling and Brian Golbey.

Sunday also sees another of the monthly "Sing and Play" sessions at the New Inn, Hurstpierpoint. As the title suggests, this is a club where the audience are expected to take an active part in the evening's entertainment.

There's good news too, concerning the "Bottle and Juggs" club who are currently meeting once a month at the City of London, London Street, Brighton. Their special guests on the 29th of this month are the Young Tradition and even more welcome news is that the club will meet weekly as from September. I hope to be able to tell you more about this newest of the local clubs next week."

The format of these regular features remained constant throughout the time that Jim wrote them. They covered a review of national and local news and artists with occasional mention of new records. There was a diary of folk events in Brighton for the next seven days and general comments on the club scene.

In 1981 however, following a change of editor, Jim was asked to make the weekly article 'more controversial' which he felt was at odds with his aims which were to present the local folk fans with an informative and factual preview of the local clubs and he 'tendered his resignation' in suitably forthright terms.

The success of Jim's articles spawned similar pieces in other Sussex papers.

The Brighton and Hove Herald introduced a Jazz Folkus column written first by John Marley and then by Jeff Rigby. On Friday 8 March 1968, following on from a piece about Jazz in Brighton and Haywards Heath Jeff wrote:

"News from the folk scene is particularly exciting this week. Tonight's meeting at the Springfield Hotel, Springfield Road, celebrates the club's fourth anniversary, and for this event they have secured an appearance by the ever-popular Alex Campbell, with a bar extension to boot.

But the main focus must be turned towards Sunday's session at the Stanford Arms, Preston Circus, when the folk club presents another scoop with a visit by one of America's most distinguished folk artists.

He is Blaine Smith, a 52-year-old singer and collector from Harrison, Virginia, who has been travelling the deep mountain region of the Southern States for the last 30 years. Blaine's life is steeped in the Southern traditions of folk music, and for the past 15 years he has been featured in his own half-hour show on local radio and TV.

His songs have been recorded by many folk artists, including the legendary Carter family, with whom he is intimately acquainted. He possesses a large repertoire and is renowned for his sense of humour, and tales and anecdotes of the Deep South. His British trip is only a short one, and the Stanford have been lucky to obtain him. All lovers of folk music are strongly recommended not to miss him."

A little later, at the end of 1969, Vic Smith, concerned by the fact that folk was then receiving only passing mention in the jazz column of the Brighton and Hove Herald, followed Jim's example and contacted the paper. The response was similar to that which Jim had received and so Vic too became a folk correspondent with a weekly report on guests appearing local clubs. The first article appeared on 19 December 1969 and continued until 30 September 1972 when publication of the paper ceased. Initially the articles were illustrated with a photograph of one of the performers mentioned, frequently a local artiste, but as the months passed the pictures became less frequent.

Meanwhile, in Lewes, Chris Duff was writing a folk column for the Mid Sussex Times but soon after the 'Brighton Herald' ceased publication he decided to take ostensibly a one year sabbatical and on 23 March 1972 Vic took over the job of writing his article. From a simple write up of guest singers in local folk clubs the column evolved into a major weekly article on the Sussex music scene, complete with illustrations, and under the title 'Music for the many' covered jazz and folk clubs in Haywards Heath, Burgess Hill, Eastbourne and Lewes as well as the Brighton conurbation, together with a range of concerts. This continued until 24 March 1981 since Chris never returned. After this, from 1981 to 1988, Vic and Tina wrote articles alternate weeks for the Sussex Express.

Jim, however, summarised a problem that no amount of advertising managed to overcome in his article on 11 November 1972 when he wrote:

"Stayaways will miss a lot

IF LOCAL folk club audiences have a fault it's the fact that they're probably a little bit too choosy in what they want to see. Don't get me wrong, though, for I don't mean that they ought to support singers of a low standard. What I'm really getting at is the certainty that if a club decides to bring a new name to the area local clubgoers tend to stay away in great numbers, preferring to turn up only when a club is featuring a well known performer.

I can think of many excellent singers whose first local appearance has been an artistic success but a disaster as far as attendance is concerned. If the folk club scene is to progress it has to have new blood. It can't exist on a diet of well-tried names, even if they are brilliant performers.

Many of the new up-and-coming names are often better value than the true and tried so-called stars, so this is tantamount to an appeal to all folk enthusiasts in the area to support their own particular club when a new singer is booked to appear. None of the club secretaries in this area knowingly engage a bad performer and you could, of course, be witnessing the early stages of a future star performer."

Much later, in the mid 90's, when I took over the organising of the Wellington folk club in Seaford I tried and was again successful, in getting coverage in the local paper the Seaford Gazette. The paper was willing to publish a report of the previous week's event, provided it had local interest and would also mention the following week's star guests. Typical was a report in March 1996.

"The appearance of Martyn Wyndham-Read, acknowledged as one of the country's foremost folk performers, brought a near capacity crowd to Seaford Folk Club in The Wellington, Steyne Road last Friday [1 March].

Martyn's repertoire for the evening covered a wide range of traditional and contemporary song from around the world together with a selection of hilarious 'bush' poems he learnt whilst living in Australia.

Support artistes were Ron Spicer, Frank Purcell, Maria Cunningham, Peter and Daphne Hawkins, Dave Middleton, Justin Grimshaw and the club's residents Mary Barr, Hazel Rose, Clive Bennett and Rigmarole.

This week the club presents the Irish singer Sean Burke, making his first appearance in Sussex, together with Jim Cochrane".

Local Radio

Although BBC Radio Brighton included some folk song in its programming this was usually an oddment rather than a regular feature apart, that is, from a Saturday morning children's programme 'Cabbages and Kings' featuring Miles Wootton.

On 23 March 1968 Jim Marshall's weekly article in the Brighton and Hove Gazette covered a rare 'Come-All-Ye' evening at the Stanford Folk Club the following Sunday, *"but with a noticeable difference!"*

"With so much excellent talent being found in the clubs these days with very few people outside being able to hear it, the entire evening on Sunday is being recorded for posterity. The main idea, however, is, if the standard is high enough, to submit an edited version to Radio Brighton in the hope that they can make use of it.

In charge of the complicated job of getting the club atmosphere on to tape is Dennis Baverstock who, besides being an ex committee member of the Stanford club is also responsible for producing taped magazines for blind members of a world-wide tape recording organisation, so all singers will be in good hands."

Subsequently Jim wrote to the BBC local radio station "Radio Brighton" suggesting they should provide more coverage of folk music which was being catered for only occasionally as part of their 'Worth Hearing' programme. Their reply was to invite him to provide suitable material for transmission since they, like the local press, had no one 'in house' to do it. As a result he started to produce tape recordings at home, including interviews made on a portable tape recorder, along with items of recorded music. This he then delivered to the studio for a monthly 15-minute item called "Folk Fifteen". This ran for thirty-four months from December 1968 but was replaced in the autumn of 1971 by

"Minstrels' Gallery" a weekly folk magazine initially lasting half an hour but later expanded to a full hour.

The production team was also enlarged to include Jim, Vic and Tina Smith and, in April 1972, Miles Wootton. This went on to become the longest running folk programme on British radio.

BBC Radio Brighton studios:
Jim Marshall 'recording'
Jim Marshall

The pilot programme was recorded, again, in Jim Marshall's front room and the opening programme, transmitted on 13 September 1971 included Brian Golbey singing "Mary of the Wild Moor" along with reviews of albums by Martyn Wyndham-Read and The Truggs.

Vic and Tina Smith 'recording'
at BBC Radio Brighton studios
Jim Marshall

The series ran for almost 25 years with Jim and Vic providing continuity for the whole period although both Tina and Miles left the production group and were replaced at various times by John Collyer, Mark Dobson, Eddie Upton, Malcolm Hayday, John Magill, Alan Jones and from 1989, for the final seven years, Tim Kent.

It survived various station name changes from Radio Brighton to Radio Sussex then Surrey and Sussex and finally Southern Counties. Only in 1996 did transmission stop and the final programme went out on 26 February 1996 by when, despite being still recorded at the studios in Marlborough Place, Brighton, it was only being broadcast by BBC Radio Solent and BBC Radio Berkshire. During its life Minstrels' Gallery featured virtually every resident singer in the area along with many of the clubs varied guests.

To the listener all seemed polished and professional and indeed, to many guests being interviewed the same applied but there was another side as can be seen by the 'photos of Jim and Vic at work editing the tapes.

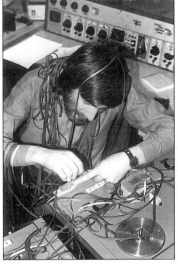

Jim Marshall and Vic Smith 'editing' tapes at BBC Radio Brighton *Jim Marshall*

This was not to be Jim Marshall's only involvement in local radio as he became the producer and regular contributor to "*South Coast Country*" hosted by Neil Coppendale until 1988. Two years later Jim returned as sole presenter and producer of the now renamed "*That's Country*" which, like "Minstrels' Gallery" ran until February 1996.

The information presented via both newspapers and radio was, since these were mass media rather than minority interest outlets, generally and naturally about the major artistes appearing in the area, particularly Brighton, during the forthcoming weeks. This again, naturally, tended to centre on the major clubs although both Jim and Vic always ensured there was mention of other clubs including some quite small events.

Whilst there was, as mentioned earlier, a very friendly relationship between the local clubs it is of course also true that you can't please all of the people all of the time. After some twenty-two years the local scene had its first and only public agitation. In June 1983 Brian Dowdall, organiser of the relatively small and broad based Monday evening folk sessions at the Dewdrop in Peacehaven, circulated a handbill inviting copy for a new folk magazine '*The Rumbler*' that, in addition to advertisements of forthcoming club guests, would provide an alternative forum for news, views and debate. It suggested that *"The major clubs in the area are not getting a proper representation in the media. You can help to correct the situation and give better coverage to many major talents by way of reasoned argument and presentation of the true facts to those who seek to present a representative presentation presently in their programmes and newspapers. Some of us are pretty tired of being left out of events on local radio etc. because of the narrow tastes of the presenters and dismissal of any form not agreeing with the tired old norm, let us make a new START."*

Printed and published by Brian each issue had a different 'guest' editor. The first issue appeared in August 1983 and Ian Fyvie, in its first editorial 'Up Front' wrote *"Welcome to 'Rumbler'! Welcome also to the chance to air controversial points of view to clear away the entrenched positions that a stifling media only fosters.*

Rumbler is to be both a forum and a shop window for acoustic arts in Sussex generally but its origins are rooted firm in the Brighton area folk scene. This first edition reflects views, comment and news of such in the knowledge that it will be inspiration to wider and more varied comment."

In addition to the 'Up Front' editorial there was a 'Readerspot' for short letters, an 'Extended Spot' for longer debate on specific topics, a 'Newsline', 'Cartoons', a 'Poet Break' for aspiring writers, a section for songs – 'Songwriter' and club's guest listings.

In the same issue was a letter from Peter Dommen, organiser of the Royal Oak Folk Club in Lewes who wrote:

"It is very pleasing to have a vehicle locally for presenting one's views and ideas regarding the local music scene. Long may it flourish within limits it can only do good.

The question of limits is largely what has caused me to put pen to paper at this early stage. It is important in the very beginning to determine what is the purpose of this new publication. On reading the preliminary handout it would appear that the prime aim was to knock the local media, however I cannot believe that this is the idea.

Questions raised by the handout can best be answered on a personal basis, so here are my <u>personal</u> views.

In the year that I have been organising a folk club the Sussex Express, Evening Argus and Radio Brighton have all regularly given space to the guests appearing. Indeed prior to forming the club the Express gave advance publicity and even went so far as to comment very favourably on the opening night in the following week's edition. From the above it is clear that personally I have no axe to grind regarding the treatment received from the media.

It is obviously not possible for me to speak for other clubs or organisers, however one should consider what action is needed if one is dissatisfied with any aspect of the local scene. I would venture to suggest that the answer is not to issue handouts full of generalisations but to discuss the problem real or imaginary with the persons supposedly at fault. We all know on a personal level the people responsible for coverage of the local folk scene, they are hardly aloof and un approachable are they?

On the subject of 'the narrow tastes of the presenters' during the last few months I have seen and heard reports or references to, Jo Ann Kelly and Pete Emery, The Taverners, Nick Dow, Jim Bainbridge, Tom Wolf and The Wolf Pack, Vic Gammon, Packie Byrne and Bonnie Shaljean, Telham Tinkers, Eddie Upton, Southdown Morris, Malcolm Austin, Roger Watson, Martin Simpson, Vin Garbutt etc, etc, etc, hardly a collection of names that one could read and then label collectively 'narrow'.

Any publication that sets out to be controversial can be fine but not if it is controversial for the sake of being so."

There were four further bi monthly issues up to April 1984 edited respectively by Peter Dommen, Martin Shough, Vic Smith and Brian and Margaret Dowdall and a further issue in the summer of that year edited by Daryl Hawkins. They contained discussions about what constituted a folk club, letters on a variety of subjects, an exchange of views by Eddie Upton and Vic Gammon and an article by Vic Smith on communication. Unfortunately there were further 'anonymous' comments about a major local club which drew a letter from Val Wagstaff, published in the final issue, number 6 "*Enough is enough! This continued sniping at one particular club and its organiser should cease.*

Those people who had criticisms to make have made them and so hopefully having got that off their chests, they'll put their energies into their music.

Jim Marshall runs his club the way he wants to and he doesn't go around telling other people how to run their clubs. Further more I'd like to know of a person in the area who has done more for folk music than Jim.

For starters, he and the other presenters and producers of Minstrels' Gallery do not get paid and have willingly given up four hours a week to promote Folk Music on Radio Sussex for the last 12 years. During that time over 100 performers have appeared in the programme.

The Sussex Folk Diary is in it's 16th year and is produced by Jim Marshall and Vic Smith. Again this has a considerable time commitment and no financial reward.

For those who don't know, Jim was in the forefront of discussions and is involved in the running of the Monday night singarounds at the Queens Head. It was a joint venture by the Friday and Sunday Springfield clubs.

How many people are aware of the fact that Jim is also Chairman of the British Country Music Association- he is also involved in the country music programme "South Coast Country" on radio Sussex.

As for the club that Jim runs on Sunday nights, did the snipers try to get in when Swarbrick and Nicol or Martin Carthy were there? Ask the 150 people in the audience if they value the Sunday club. So it's not like that every week, so what! Finally in all the letters and comments over the last nine months it seems to me that the one person who has emerged with any dignity is Jim Marshall."

Publicity

At a more parochial level, towards the end of 1969, although the publicity material produced by individual clubs had achieved quite a professional appearance, the volume was so great that it 'cluttered up' the entrance of each club.

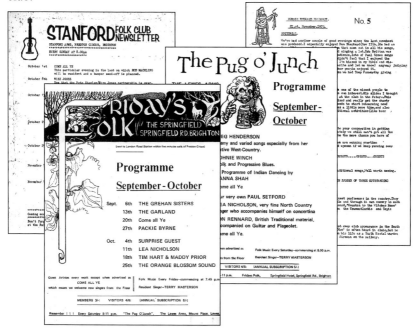

**Selection of pre 1970 folk club leaflets: the Author and Terry Masterson
Stanford, Friday's Folk, Pug O' Junch and Merrie England**

To address this problem Jim Marshall [Stanford Arms Sunday Club] and Vic and Tina Smith [Marlborough Tuesday club], supported by Paul Setford [Springfield Friday club], agreed to collaborate in the production of a bi-monthly diary of guest performers at the towns folk clubs – ***The Brighton Folk Diary*** – *'A Free Guide to Local Folk Clubs'*.

Issue No.1, covering the guests at these three clubs for January and February 1970 rapidly expanded and No.2 added Cuthbert Toad Hall and the

University of Sussex Folk Clubs in Brighton along with the Pug O' Junch club in Lewes. Further expansions led to the inclusion of most of the clubs in Sussex and by issue 12 it had become 'The Free Guide to Sussex Folk Clubs'. In March 1973, after 19 issues, it became the 'Sussex Folk Diary'.

Then from January 1986 [Issue 96] simply '*The Folk Diary*' – a publication still available today [Issue 195 – June/July 2002] and still produced, after 32 years, by Jim Marshall and Vic Smith.

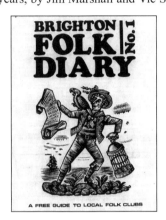

Folk Diary Cover. Nos. 1 and 172
the author

Apart from the listing of guest singers at the clubs the early editions included pen pictures of the both guests and some resident performers – Terry Masterson, Miles Wootton and Paul Setford – and there was an occasional song. This started in issue No 5 with 'Swallow, Swallow' by Miles Wootton and Allan Taylor followed in No.9 with the ballad 'The Wife of Ushers Well'. There was, after the second issue, an editorial 'I Say, I Say' with information or comments on the local scene written by either Jim or Vic. The first 'I Say, I Say' editorial explained:

"Why have we waited until the third issue of Brighton Folk Diary before we published an editorial? Well, it's really all a matter of finance. In the two previous editions there hasn't been any spare space, but we're happy to say that, with the kind help of our advertisers, we've been able to increase the number of pages to sixteen with the result that we have room to expand.

Elsewhere in the Diary you'll find the first of an occasional series on local folk singers and we hope to be in a position to feature news and record reviews in future issues, providing we get the all too necessary advertising revenue.

The Diary was originally started with the idea of doing away with all those sundry leaflets which littered the paying-in table at all local clubs and, although there still are some loose leaflets about, we feel that by collating most of them into one publication we've tidied things up quite a bit and, in the process, produced a worthwhile magazine.

However, if the Diary is to continue and expand we need your help, both for advice and advertising. If you can help in any way, please let us know. Our advertising rates are probably the lowest anywhere and, remember, with a life of two months, the Diary keeps your advert in the public eye that much longer than other publications. . "

Expansion was rapid and clubs well beyond Brighton were soon using its pages for publicity. This was reflected in 'I Say, I Say' where news from around the county started to appear. In issue 12 Jim Marshall wrote:

"Well, they said we'd never make it, but here we are completing our second year of publication with what we hope is our most ambitious edition so far.

A great deal has happened in recent months on the local folk scene, so it might be a good opportunity to mention some of the more notable changes.

Biggest shock was the unexpected closure of Cuthbert Toad hall club. This rather unique establishment did much to attract young people to the folk movement and I'm sure its ever-active secretary, Audrey Judd, will soon be back in business in some form or other.

Newer clubs include Bryan Blanchard's popular Sunday session at Horsham and those at the Clarence in Hastings whose secretary, Linda Gowans, has recently also taken on the duties of resident along with Peter Cunningham.

John Bassett's a fairly regular singer in most Brighton area clubs and now he's opening his own at the Marlborough. At present it has to be alternate Thursdays, but John hopes to make it weekly in the New Year. This, of course, in no way affects the monthly Sunday 'Guitar at the Marlborough' evenings.

Neil Coppendale's Country and Western club opened with a bang at the Richmond Hotel in Brighton in September and seems set for sure success with some top names booked to appear.

A 'soft music' club opened at the Imperial in Queens Road in September, but the pub's now been sold, so the club's organiser, Paul Carpenter, is frantically looking for alternative premises to re-open this mainly contemporary club. By the time you read this he may be back in business.

One's tempted to ask Bob Copper why he's never got around to running his own club before, despite the fact that there have been the occasional Copper Nights. The answer, of course, is that Bob's a very busy man, but he has finally decided to hold a regular monthly session at his Peacehaven club. With Seamus Ennis on the opening night, it's assured of a great send-off.

Radio Brighton's new folk programme, "Minstrel's Gallery" got off to a flying start in September and continues to be heard every other Monday evening at 6.30 pm., featuring local and national talent, record reviews and news. Dates for the rest of this year are October 25, November 8 and 22, December 6 and 20.

If you were lucky enough to see the Chithurst Mummers' play last year, you'll be delighted to hear that an entirely new production will be presented again this year with a couple of performances in aid of the Evening Argus Christmas Appeal, at the Lewes Arms in Lewes and the Stanford Arms, Brighton. Please support this exceptionally worthy cause. If last year's performances were anything to go by, you can safely go and see both the Lewes and Stanford productions, as the wholesale ad-libbing makes no two shows alike.

It's difficult to list what are expected to be the highlights of the coming months in the clubs, but visits from Seamus Ennis, Therapy, Bob Davenport, Tim Hart and Maddy Prior, Lea Nicholson, Bill Clifton, Allan Taylor add up to some top-line talent and a newish traditional duo at the Hastings club, called Caldbec Hill, sound extremely interesting. However, take a good look at all the club details in this issue, for whether they're big names or not, you can always count on local organisers to present the best in folk entertainment."

It was at about this time that the 'Folk Boom' was in full swing in the Brighton area, as Vic Smith noted in the Brighton and Hove Herald on 27 February 1970.

"It is fairly obvious to anyone interested in the local folk scene that Brighton is experiencing a boom at the moment. I make it 12 weekly folk song meetings against four this time last year. Not all are having a happy time financially at the moment, and it may be that some rationalisation may come about.

It is interesting to compare these local figures with Leeds where there are now four clubs against 23 two years ago.

One feature of this boom is that popular artists appear in the area more frequently:"

The effect was of course that more and more clubs advertised in the Diary and circulation increased. The spin off was that as the publication became more established so commercial advertising was added from breweries, record companies, instrument shops and national folk events. The extent to which it expanded in a relatively short space of time was illustrated in issue 17 when Vic wrote in 'I Say, I Say':

"In Brighton Folk Diary number 16 we had 17 clubs advertising their programme and we thought that we then had a comprehensive guide to clubs in the area. However, we were wrong, for this time we welcome Stan Wigg's soon-to-open venture at Washington and the Brighton College of Education Club. Previously this latter club met in the college at Falmer, but, in an attempt to diversify their audience, they are going to meet in future at the Pier which has long been a popular pub for live music.

The Horsham club is on the move in September. With the demolition of the "Swan", the club loses a fine room and the most genial of landlords. Bryan Blanchard tells me that their new premises, the "Anchor" in East Street, offers a larger room, which is some compensation.

Changes, too, on the airwaves. From September 2nd, BBC radio Brighton goes on to Medium Wave at 202 metres. As well as extending coverage in Brighton itself, the new frequency should considerably widen the range of the station to the north of the Downs. The VHF spot remains at 95.8 MHz. . . . . . ".

In January 1976 the editorial was re-titled 'Soapbox' and opened up for articles from guest writers including Vic Gammon, John Towner from the Telham club, Fred Woods – editor of the national magazine 'Folk Review', Stuart Reed of the Taverners, Mary Aitchison – editor of the Sussex folk magazine 'Plum Heavy', Tony Wales – founder of the Horsham Songswappers, local singers Paul Hawes, Miles Wootton, Jerry Jordan, Warwick Downes and Eddie Upton, club organisers Brian Dowdall of Peacehaven and Val Wagstaff from Friday's Folk and Harry Mousdell from Horsham.

'Soapbox' ended in September 1982 and was replaced a year later in August 1983 by an occasional 'Comment' but the last of these appeared in October 1984. The new format of the Diary, introduced in December 1985 included items of folk news and 'Turntable' a review of folk records – a feature still to be found in the Diary today although it is now called 'New Albums'.

Possibly the best way to follow what has happened in and around the town since January 1970 is to thumb through the back numbers of this comprehensive guide to the local folk scene augmented with the more detailed articles published in the Brighton and Hove Gazette from 1969 to 1981.

Today 'The Diary' arrives at Jim's home ready for distribution but in earlier times, as many club regulars will recall, there was always a request for assistance to collate and staple them ready for distribution. There were always a number of volunteers to 'work' under the watchful eyes of Jim and Vic but the task normally took a whole evening.

Collating 'the Diary'. Jim and Vic with Andy Miller – a regular – and other members of the 'team' in Tina and Vic's house, Brighton
Jim Marshall

The early stapling sessions were in Laurence and Sandra Goddard's flat in Eaton Place, Kemp Town or Vic and Tina's house in Stanmer Villas, Brighton where, if their visit coincided with a new issue of the Diary, Tina's parents would be among the 'volunteers'. Later these sessions were transferred to the clubrooms at The Springfield and The

Royal Oak, Lewes. Tina's father, an avid reader, was incidentally responsible for providing some of Roger Brasier's material.

As Jim noted in SOAPBOX the 'editorial' of the Sussex Folk Diary No. 46 for July and August 1977:

"This is the one issue of the Diary which I don't have to help collate and staple, so it's perhaps a suitable occasion for me to issue a word of thanks to all those willing slaves who regularly offer their services for this particular exciting task. 18,000 sheets of paper waiting to be transformed into 3,000 copies of the magazine is a daunting sight, even to old stagers like me who've been in on it since issue number one. The help is greatly appreciated and if there are any other volunteers for this bi-monthly task, please let us know and we'll accept your offer gladly."

Virtually all the issues from number 1 to 95 featured a pictorial cover, usually selected by Jim from a host of cuttings and illustrations he accumulated for the purpose. However from 1974 to 77 the covers of fifteen issues between 25 and 51 featured original artwork created by Lawrence Heath.

In crediting the above design in 'I Say, I Say' of issue No. 33 of The Diary Jim Marshall wrote:

"Once again we are very grateful to Lawrence Heath for an excellent front cover. This one illustrates a fourteenth century legend. Lady Edona is standing on top of St. Nicholas Hill in Brighton, watching the ship of Lord Manfred, her husband-to-be. As a result of a curse, the ship goes down and he is drowned. On the anniversary of the sinking, the story goes, a ghost ship can be seen. So look out from the Dyke Road area on May 17th ".

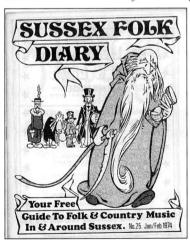 

Sussex Folk Diary No. 25   **Sussex Folk Diary No. 33**
Covers by Lawrence Heath *the author*

In December 1999, as the century closed, the Folk Diary issue No.180 celebrated its 30th year of publication, reproducing on the back page the cover and three club adverts from the first issue.

One issue later the first of the new millennium, there was a rather sad footnote bidding goodbye to the Stanford Arms, the one time coaching inn built in 1874 which had played host to Brighton's major folk club from the early 60's to the mid 1970's. The pub had closed in November and re-opened, complete with neon signs, a few weeks later as a somewhat stark and uninviting coffee bar called 'Circus, Circus'. Such is progress.

6 SPECIAL EVENTS
CONCERTS, FESTIVALS AND FOLK DAYS

In Brighton, like most towns, there may occasionally have been some slight sense of rivalry between clubs but it was insignificant and far overshadowed by the degree of co-operation between the different factions. The lack of conflict spread right across the scene covering the club organisers, residents and audience many of whom regularly visited each other's clubs. Each of the major clubs appeared to have an individual style, the Sunday club was generally viewed as broad based with a tendency towards commercial and American folk, Friday's Folk was seen as traditional as was Lewes. Looking at the guest list however shows this to have been largely an illusion. Each of the long running clubs mentioned featured a good cross section of established guest singers although the various residents possibly fitted more closely to the perceived club style. The high level of contact between club organisers included liaison from time to time to avoid conflicting star guest bookings and on one auspicious occasion to combine for a tour by Martin Carthy. That was in 1975 when Martin appeared, on each occasion to a packed audience, at Friday's Folk on 19 September, the Lewes Arms the following night and the Stanford on Sunday 21st. The friendship, particularly between the three major clubs, is perhaps best shown by their collaboration in producing the Folk Diary, an enduring sign of joint ventures. Beyond this however there have been others ventures both commercial and social starting as early as 1966.

Home Spun 1966
In April 1966 John Eccles of the Brighton and Hove Herald reported that he had *"learnt the secret ambition of every Brighton folk organiser . . . to put on a folk concert at the Dome and feature local folk artists to a capacity crowd."*

Then, quoting Jack Whyte, as saying *"We have the talent to bring the house down I'm sure."* John went on to say, *"To this end Jack is already laying plans with other folk leaders."* Again quoting Jack he added *"It's an ambition of mine to put on a concert of this nature. Would we fill the Dome without advertising a celebrity? . . . I doubt it. But I am certain that the talent of our local singers would thrill any audience we could cajole into visiting the Dome."*

Thus was the stage set for the first event to include members of 'rival' clubs. This took place on 8 November 1966 in the form of a concert at the Dome. Initially, as shown, it was Jack Whyte's idea but Jack, Terry Masterson and Miles Wootton staged the actual event as a joint venture. The organisers didn't risk running without star guests but whilst Nadia Cattouse, Martin Carthy and Dave Swarbrick were booked as the top names the line up of local singers was impressive with Jack Whyte, Terry Masterson, Paul Setford and 'The Halliards' – Derek Lockwood, Eddie Upton and Paul Holden from Friday's Folk at the Springfield and Rod Machling, Brian Golbey and Mel and Miles from the Brighton Singers Club at the Stanford. Incidentally, although billed as the Halliards, the group had been renamed The Juggs by the time the concert actually took place.

a Concert of FOLK MUSIC
at THE DOME
Tuesday 8th November 7.30
MARTIN CARTHY
DAVE SWARBRICK
NADIA CATTOUSE

tickets : 10¹6 7¹6 6¹- 5¹-
Dome Booking Office - New Road

HOME SPUN

'Home Spun' concert ticket 1966 *Jim Marshall*

This easy inter relationship between the club organisers persisted and in time gave rise to purely social events with Christmas Dinners and eventually a reunion party.

Christmas Dinners

Many of the club organisers and residents from Brighton during the late 1970's held an annual Christmas get together and dinner at the Springfield. When the long term and friendly landlord and landlady Jim and Heather Keelty, moved to Keymer the folk enthusiasts followed them and on 9 December 1980 held another Christmas celebration, this time at The Thatched Inn, Keymer. It was a great success and repeated the following year.

Sussex Folk Clubs Dinner 1983 *[left to right]* **Jim Marshall, John Ticehurst, Laurie Goddard, Val Wagstaff, George Wagstaff, the author, guest, Colin Baker, Rebe Upton, Eddie Upton.**
Jim Marshall

Next year however it was arranged after Christmas and to accommodate the increasing number of people who wanted to attend the event was held in the Café de Paris, St James's Street, Brighton where, on 4 January 1983, they took over the whole restaurant for the evening. Again a great success it was repeated on 11 January 1984.

**Menu from Café de Paris,
Brighton 1983** *Jim Marshall*

Folk Reunion Party

The most recent 'joint' venture was an all day long reunion party held at the Royal Oak, Lewes on Saturday 22 October 1994. Organised by Vic and Tina Smith and Jim Marshall it was based on a suggestion by Brian Golbey. As Jim and Vic wrote in Folk Diary No.150 for December 1990:

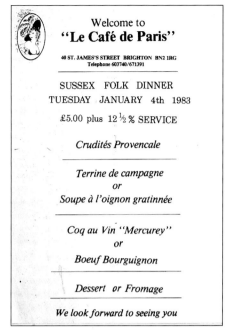

Welcome to
"Le Café de Paris"

40 ST. JAMES'S STREET BRIGHTON BN2 1RG
Telephone 603740/671391

SUSSEX   FOLK   DINNER
TUESDAY   JANUARY   4th   1983

£5.00 plus 12 ½ % SERVICE

Crudités Provencale

Terrine de campagne
or
Soupe à l'oignon gratinnée

Coq au Vin "Mercurey"
or
Boeuf Bourguignon

Dessert or Fromage

We look forward to seeing you

*"**Wasn't That A Party**. It was Brian Golbey's idea in the first place. He mentioned that whenever he came back to Sussex for a gig, from his home in Nottingham, he only ever had time to say a quick 'hello' and 'goodbye' to his many friends from the days when he was a Brighton club resident. 'How about an all-day social get-together?' he asked, so we thought about it for a couple on minutes and decided it was worth a try.*

Saturday October 22nd was the chosen day, the Royal Oak in Lewes the venue. We weren't sure whether anyone would turn up, but the whole thing turned out to be a huge success with people arriving from all over the place – from Northern Island, Germany and even Ringmer! People we'd not seen, in some cases, for fifteen or twenty years. Lovely to see them all again.

The afternoon, from midday, was mainly spent nattering about the old days, as you'd expect. There was a fair bit of music then, but it was in the evening that things really got going. One song each was the order of the day and, even then, many people didn't get a chance to do their stuff. The wag who said that nostalgia isn't what it used to be had better think again.

Will we do it again? Certainly! Watch this space."

Club 'Specials' and Concerts

At the peak of the folk 'boom' in the 1970's there were so many clubs vying for the services of top name performers that it was not always possible to book a particular artiste on the night your club met. Alternatively, the organiser might be offered the services of a touring singer on a particular day, which was not the club night. Jim Marshall's response was to adopt an

131

unusual degree of flexibility. He staged a 'special' evening, initially as an extra club night and later in the form of a concert.

Jim's first foray into alternative evenings was on Wednesday 4 August 1969 and featured Reverend Gary Davis who was visiting England to appear at the Cambridge Folk Festival. Later, on Wednesday 27 May 1970, the Stanford club ran a charity evening in aid of the Royal National Institute for the Blind with residents from all the local clubs volunteering their services free. These included Tim Broadbent, Roger Hubbard, Terry Masterson, Vic and Tina Smith, Roger Brasier, Peter Collins, Keith Johns, Rod Machling and Miles Wootton. A week later on Wednesday 3 June the club staged another special guest evening with Michael Cooney from the U.S.A.

The next event was in a sense accidental. Jake Thackray was scheduled to appear at the Stanford on Sunday 27 September but had to cancel at the last minute due to illness. A new date was quickly arranged as an 'Evening with Jake Thackray' on Wednesday 18 November, which drew a capacity audience to the clubroom.

Encouraged by the response Jim arranged another Jake Thackray special the following year on Saturday 30 October 1971 but this time at the Gardner Centre at Sussex University with club residents Tim Broadbent, Miles Wootton and Marie Curtis as support artistes. Admission was 60 pence unreserved and 45 pence students, OAP's and Stanford club members. The format was repeated a few months later, again at the Gardner Centre, on 26 February 1972 with Jeremy Taylor as the star guest. 16 December 1972, again on a Saturday, and again at the Gardner Centre saw a third Jake Thackray special this time supported by Roger Brasier, Terry Masterson and Miles Wootton.

On Tuesday 18 September 1973 Jim continued with the concert idea when he used the Wagner Hall, Regency Road, Brighton to present Boys of the Lough, Martin Carthy and Swan Arcade. For such a superb line up tickets were a modest 75 pence each. This was the third part of a triple bill, as Jim noted in the Folk Diary 'I Say, I Say':

"All of a sudden it's all happening at the Wagner Hall in Brighton, with three concerts within the space of one week in September. For a start Jake Thackray appears in a show which is being promoted and recorded by BBC Radio Brighton and that's on Wednesday September 12th followed a couple of days later, on Friday 14th September with the Brighton début of Sounds of Nashville, a fantastic, mainly American, country band, with an attractive girl singer and a brilliant steel-guitarist in the person of Brian Williams who's no stranger to Brighton audiences. Sounds of Nashville replaces the previously advertised appearance of Tracy Miller who has now cancelled her British tour.

The third in the trio of concerts is on Tuesday September 18th and features the Boys of the Lough, Martin Carthy and Swan Arcade. Beat that for a line up!

In case you're not familiar with the Wagner Hall, it's a brand new building in Regency Road, which is the second turning off West Street on the right hand side going from the Clock Tower. It has excellent facilities and is ideal for folk events."

Wagner Hall concert poster 1973
Jim Marshall

Concerts appeared to be popular and on Friday 2 November the Gardner Centre itself entered the folk world with a concert by the Yetties. The following year, on 27 March 1974, Vic Smith staged a concert at the Wagner Hall featuring Allan Taylor and Martyn Wyndham-Read.

Jim however returned to club based specials when, on Monday 23 September 1974, Boys of the Lough appeared at the Stanford, followed on Wednesday 8 September 1976, again at the Stanford, with John Renbourn and Jacqui McShee. Admission was 70 pence. The next Stanford 'specials' were in the summer of 1977 when Jim organised a 'long weekend' of folk with an extra meeting either side of the regular club session. Jake Thackray appeared on Thursday 21 July with Martin Carthy at the Sunday meeting and John Renbourn completing the line up on Tuesday 26. This was followed in the autumn by a special appeal event on Wednesday 5 October featuring local singers to raise funds for Dave Goulder who had suffered a disastrous fire which had destroyed his Scottish croft and all its contents. There were to be three more Stanford Sunday club specials. The first on Wednesday 9 April 1980 featured Ossian and the next, a few months later on Wednesday 30 July presented Martin Carthy with three friends from the U.S.A. – Jody Stecher, Krishna Bhatt and Hank Bradley – who played traditional American country music. The final special was at the King Alfred restaurant, Kingsway, Hove and featured long time favourite Jake Thackray. Admission was now £2.00.

Concerts were not entirely out of fashion and the Gardner Centre staged several folk events. Notably Boys of the Lough appeared there in March

133

1975 and again in November 1981. Then there was an Albion Band Christmas show in December 1984 and a triple-header in October 1985 with Leon Rosselson, Frankie Armstrong and Roy Bailey. Two other events with a local flavour were Brighton Folk on Saturday 19 July 1980 featuring Shirley Collins with Stuart Reed, Christine Hase, Eddie Upton and the Pump and Pluck Band, Uncle John's Band, Roger Brasier and Little Edith's Treat and then a concert by Arizona Smoke Revue on Tuesday 15 February 1983 with John Collyer, Christine Hase, Terry Masterson and Alan White providing the support and Stuart Reed acting as compère. In 1985, on Saturday 18 May, Peter Dommen organised a concert at Lewes priory Middle School in Mountfield Road featuring Julie Felix supported by Terry Masterson and The Taverners.

Later, in 1990, when Jim Marshall had re-opened a folk club at the Stanford Arms on Friday evenings he again staged a 'special' on Saturday 6 October featuring Martin Carthy and Dave Swarbrick with Anne Briggs.

LOCAL FESTIVALS AND FOLK DAYS

The first local folk 'festival' was the 'Brighton Folk Music Festival', sponsored by the English Folk Dance and Song Society and organised by Paul Setford, at the Co-op Hall in London Road on 10 September 1966 a few weeks before the 'Home Spun' concert at the Dome, mentioned earlier. The EFDSS News dated July 1966 reported *"The Festival is being arranged by the Sussex District, at the Co-operative Hall, London Road, Brighton. It is designed to be an informal gathering with opportunities for all singers and instrumentalists attending to take part. Plus some special guest performers. Sessions: 3-6 p.m. and 7-10.30 p.m."*

This was followed, on 21 October 1967, by a similar event at the Ralli Hall, Hove. Again sponsored by the EFDSS and organised by Paul Setford.

On the day before the event Jim Marshall's folk column in The Brighton and Hove Gazette noted: *"The Ralli Hall, next to Hove station, is the scene of this year's Sussex Folk Festival, which takes place tomorrow in two sessions, one from 3pm to 6pm and the other from 7pm to 10.30*
Featured singers are Terry Masterson and Martyn Wyndham-Read but there will also be many other singers, covering all aspects of folk music from pure traditional to contemporary, including American blues and country music."

A week later in the same paper he reported: *"Last Saturday's Sussex Folk Festival in Hove turned out to be an even greater success than was anticipated. Well over 50 singers entertained a packed house almost non-stop for more than seven hours and, even then, left them shouting for more.*
It's obvious that this type of event must take place at more frequent intervals than at present. Special praise must go to Paul Setford who did the major part of the organising and kept proceedings running exceptionally smoothly."

Although the frequency of the event was not increased the size was and the following year it expanded to include club sessions on the Friday evening and Sunday. On 11 October 1968 Jim reported in his weekly folk column:

"Final Details have just been released of next month's Sussex Folk Festival. These events started out as the brain-child of local singer Paul Setford and in previous years he has been mainly responsible for their presentation. This year, however, it's a combined effort featuring the Springfield and Stanford clubs, the University of Sussex Folk Club and the English Folk Dance and Song Society and it promises to be the biggest and best festival ever held in this part of the world.

The proceedings kick off with a visit to the Springfield of ace guitarist Davy Graham. He has many imitators and this will be one of his vary rare club appearances. This will be on Friday November 1 and on the following day there'll be a marathon "Come All Ye" style concert at the Ralli Hall, Hove with both folk dance and song and featuring guest group the Yetties.

This is an afternoon and evening show and should cover every taste in folk song, from unaccompanied traditional to blues and country music.

Sunday November 3, is also a pretty full day. It starts with an afternoon session at the University of Sussex with those two excellent performers Jacqueline McDonald and Bridie O'Donnell and this is followed by the final event of the festival when the Stanford Folk Club presents Martin Carthy and Dave Swarbrick."

The event at the Ralli Hall, Hove was again sponsored by the EFDSS and featured the Coppers as guest singers.

Co-op Folk Days

The following year these festivals were superseded by the first, of what became a series, of annual Folk Days held early in July each year from 1969 to 1974 in the grounds of the Royal Pavilion, Brighton as part of the annual Co-operative International Fair.

The Brighton and Hove Gazette, on 4 July 1969, reported *"The biggest ever event organised for Co-operative Day in Brighton – the International Fair is being staged on the Royal Pavilion Lawns tomorrow. It will be opened at 2.30 by Vera Lynn. Continuous free entertainment throughout the afternoon will include the Ringmer Secondary School Band, who will play a selection of music associated with Vera Lynn before she arrives, a festival of Folk Music with local singers taking part, and demonstrations of judo, karate, kendo, ladie's keep-fit, Scottish dancing and folk dancing . . . "*

The fair was organised by Councillor Don Ranger with Vic and Tina Smith in charge of the folk singing. In 1970 the format was repeated as Jim Marshall noted in his folk column of the Brighton and Hove gazette on 3 July

1970: *" . . an item of special interest tomorrow afternoon. It's the Co-op International Fair and as part of the festivities on the lawns of the Royal Pavilion, there's an almost non-stop folk session featuring most of the best local singers. There's no admission charge, so you've no excuse not to go and lend your moral and vocal support and there's a beer tent close by!"*

A week later the same paper reported: "About 5,000 people packed the fair, the biggest and best organised by Brighton Co-operative Party, which was in aid of the Oxfam Botswana project . . ." It went on to add that the event was opened by Dick Emery.

Co-op Folk Day
[left to right]
**Ivor Pickard,
Marie Curtis,
Tina Smith, Alan
White,
Pam Fereday and
Vic Smith.**
Jim Marshall

Similar events were held on 10 July 1971, 8 July 1972 – although due to persistent rain the event was moved indoor to the Corn Exchange, 7 July 1973 and 6 July 1974 when, the following week, the Brighton and Hove Gazette reported: *" . . organised to help celebrate the 52nd International Co-operative Day the fair featured more than 70 sideshows and stalls and a free afternoon's entertainment for parents and children. About 6,000 visitors helped raise a total of over £1,000"*

Lewes Folk Day

From the Co-op folk days in Brighton Vic and Tina progressed to the Lewes Folk Day, organised, initially, as part of a Festival of Lewes.

The organisers of a Lewes Festival approached Tina and Vic to run some form of folk event as part of the festival. They came up with the idea of a Folk Day and approached Ashley Hutchings and Shirley Collins, then part of the Etchingham Steam Band. It became a joint promotion on a shared profit basis with Tina and Vic providing the major part of the organising and local administration. The Folk Day was a huge success although the rest of the festival fell short of expectations and the organisers tried, unsuccessfully, to get some of the Folk Day profits to meet their shortfall. That was the end of the

Festival but not the Folk Day which became part of the local scene for the next decade.

The first Folk Day was held on 12 July 1975 and Jim Marshall again, reporting in his Folk column of the Brighton and Hove Gazette on 5th July that year wrote: *"Although it is not exactly a folk festival, next Saturday's Lewes Folk Day is the nearest you'll get to one in this part of the country. As part of the Lewes Festival, the authorities have co operated with local clubs and singers to present almost an entire day of folk activities.*

The climax is a celidh at LEWES TOWN HALL which will run concurrently with the LEWES ARMS Folk Club, with events presenting the same artists, namely the Etchingham Steam Band and John and Sue Kirkpatrick. Others involved during the day are the Chanctonbury Ring Morris Men and the Knots Of May, the all ladies folk dance team."

On 24 July 1976 the second Folk Day was publicised as an 'All Sussex' event with featured guests including Martyn Wyndham-Read, Shirley Collins, The Coppers, Bob Lewis, George Belton and Cyril Phillips along with Chanctonbury Ring Morris Men, Knots of May and Potters Wheel with Eddie Upton as Caller. There was an afternoon family session at the Castle Lodge, Surgery Lawns along with dance displays, a Ceilidh and song club session. This was repeated on 23 July 1977 when those appearing were The Watersons, Martin Carthy, Pete & Chris Coe, The New Victory Band, Muckram Wakes and Mel Dean along with Chanctonbury Ring Morris and the Knots of May. This proved to be the biggest of the Folk days in terms of attendance. It attracted a lot of attention in the national press and many top names turned up to make 'floor' appearances, ranging from Spider John Koerner to Cilla Fisher and Artie Tresize.

In 1978 the organisers were forced to cancel the event because Lewes Town Hall was closed.

As Vic Smith explained in the Folk Diary No.51 SOAPBOX:

"The event which was planned for Saturday 22nd July this year has had to be cancelled. Lewes Town hall is scheduled for re-decoration during the summer and the District Council are still not able to say for certain when the work will commence. Anyone who has attended the event in previous years will realise the Town Hall plays a vital part in our plans for the day and without it the event would not be viable artistically or financially.

It is annoying to find that a booking arrangement that was made more than a year in advance cannot be guaranteed. It was also rather irritating to hear about the matter indirectly. If John Owen, the landlord of the Lewes Arms, had not informed me that he heard of the re-decorating plans then I could have been well advanced with the arrangements and still been faced with a cancellation.

The decision to cancel causes me disappointment on several counts. Firstly, I thoroughly enjoy the day myself and know it will be a let-down to many others who have told me how much they have enjoyed Lewes Folk day in previous years and how much they were looking forward to it this year. Then there are the artists who have been holding this date for me, also since last July.

However, I have booked the Town hall for Saturday 29th July 1979 and asked the guests booked this year if they will take part then. These are John & Sue Kirkpatrick, The Umps and Dumps, the Chanctonbury Ring Morris Men and the Knots of May. I also hope that Neil Brewer whose work with the amplification has drawn much praise from the artists, reviewers and from the audience in past years will be in charge of the sound. Any suggestions for ways of improving or for items for inclusion in Lewes Folk day 1979 would be most welcome."

For 28 July 1979 however the event was scaled down and concentrated on local singers, including The Taverners, Malcolm and Julia Donaldson, Bob Lewis, Eddie Upton, Vic Gammon, Terry Masterson, Little Edith's Treat, Maxwells Demon, The Lewes Band, Chanctonbury Ring Morris Men and Knots of May.

The following year, on 26 July, there was a mixture of 'names' both national and local with Bob Davenport, Peta Webb, Miles Wootton, Terry Masterson and Eddie Upton and then in 1981 on 25 July there was a very comprehensive guest list with Martin Carthy, John Kirkpatrick & Howard Evans, Bob Cann & Terry Potter and Band, Vic Gammon, Eddie Upton, Isabel Sutherland and Terry Masterson.

On 31 July 1982 there was another Lewes Folk Day, this time featuring the High Level Ranters, Cosmotheka, John Collyer, Catsfield Steamers and Terry Masterson.

Vic and Tina decided not to organise an event the following year. As Vic recalls *"It was not that the event was not viable. In fact every Lewes Folk Day was successful financially. The problem was that we had so many up front expenses which escalated from year to year and could only be recouped on the day of the event if enough people turned up. We had no backing."* The Lewes District Council was less than helpful, almost to the extent of being obstructive. As Vic, again, remembers *"It [Lewes DC] kept putting various high rents and insurance charges our way. I tried to get backing from South East Arts, but the best we ever got from them was: "Go ahead and hold your event and then we will talk about it afterwards if things go badly." With no guarantee of financial input."* He adds *"In effect, it was our holiday money that was invested in the event each year and we could only ever arrange a holiday at a few days' notice after we were seen to cover our expenses. Increasingly this seemed unfair on our young family."*

In the spring of 1983 however, Peter Dommen, who was co-organiser of the Sunday evening 'Folk in the Oak' sessions at the Royal Oak, decided to try and continue the event with a weekend of singing. This song-orientated festival took place on 23 and 24 July. On the Saturday there was a session in the gardens of the YMCA with an evening concert in the Priory School Hall featuring Wilbury Jam and Atholl Brose and a song session at the Brewers Arms. Then, on Sunday, the Royal Oak hosted a lunch time session with Wilbury Jam in the bar and an evening song club featuring the Taverners. The event was run on a tight budget and apart from booking Roger Watson and Martin Simpson as 'star' guests, relied largely on local singers including Fred Baxter, Ian Fyvie, Indrani and Martin, John Zarfass, George Oakley, Trevor Curry, Pat Ford, Val Wagstaff and Charlotte Oliver. It also featured Tim O'Leary and Nick Burbridge who ran Irish music sessions in Brighton pubs augmented by Tim's brother Christie who came over from Ireland for the event. Although publicity for the day's activities was rather parochial – there was no advertisement in the Folk Diary for example – support was generally good.

The following year, on the weekend 20/22 July 1984 Vic and Tina again took up the reins of organising. Fortunately, this time, they secured financial support from Radio Sussex who, in exchange for recording rights to the performers, helped underwrite the event. This enabled the organisers to book a host of top names for the weekend and featured Martin Carthy, the Oyster Band, Adrian May, Roger Watson, Jim Bainbridge, Lynn Clayton, Rosbif, Pete Stanley & Brian Golbey, Mike Draper & Cathy Locke, Vic Gammon, Oliver & Spong, Miles Wootton and Terry Masterson.

Dr. Vic Gammon and Laurie Goddard share a joke at Lewes Folk day
Jim Marshall

The following year, 1985, the event was again dropped from the folk calendar but on 26 July 1986 it once more surfaced in the capable hands of Vic and Tina with John James, the Oyster Band, Sara Grey & Ellie Ellis, Rosbif, Printers Measure, Vic Gammon and Eddie Upton as guests.

The tenth and final Lewes Folk Day was held on 25 July 1987 again organised by Vic and Tina in association with BBC Radio Sussex. The featured guests were: Gas Mark 5, Kathryn Tickell, Spring Chickens, Lea Nicholson, Dick Richardson, Mary Panton, Four Piece Suite, Tim Kent, Rob and Lu Horton, Broken Ankles, Vic Gammon and Will Duke, Knots of May and Pilgrim Morris. There was the usual children's event in the morning in the YMCA Gardens, a lunchtime singaround in the Lewes Arms and a lunchtime dance tour. This was followed by an open-air concert in the afternoon in the

YMCA Gardens and a full evening of folk entertainment with a concert in the Royal Oak, a dance at the Priory Middle School hall and a singaround in the Lewes Arms. Unfortunately Kathryn Tickell cancelled late on the Friday evening. Vic reflects that *"Many panic 'phone calls later and we were able to call on Peta Webb and Pete Cooper who gave a tremendously professional performance considering they had less than 12 hours notice."*

In many ways the Lewes Folk Days represented the high point of the co-operation which has been a feature of the Sussex and particularly Brighton, folk scene for some forty years. Vic and Tina summed it up, saying: *"They were a great deal of work* [for us] *and we tried to tie up all the organisational details in advance, but we got a tremendous amount of help and support from a great number of people who acted as marshals, compères, money takers and collectors and also helped*

accommodate the visiting guest artists. Particular mention should be made of Laurie Goddard and Jim Marshall who spent many hours on the doors and entrances taking money and checking tickets and Rebe Cleveland who was a very efficient treasurer."

Colin Baker and Jill Hockmuth at Lewes Folk Day 1987 *Tim Kent*

Brighton International Folk Festival – September 1977

Between the 1977 and 1979 Lewes Folk Days there was something that might best be described as a non-event, the first and only, Brighton International Folk Festival. Although not organised by the local clubs it was an event that should surely have been a great success, given the line up of guest artistes and the strong local support for folk music. Unfortunately it serves as a cautionary tale for would be impresarios.

For the 2-4 September 1977, as the first public event to be held in the brand new Brighton Centre, Fred Woods, former Editor of 'Folk Review' the country's major folk magazine, decided to organise a weekend festival headed by Burl Ives, one of the foremost names of the folk revival, supported by a veritable who's who of the British folk scene.

The format included three evening concerts in the Main Hall and various related activities in other parts of the building, which included folk entertainment by Taffy Thomas and Tony 'Doc' Shiels. In addition both

Chanctonbury Ring and Broadwood Morris Men danced inside the hall and outside in Churchill Square and by the Palace Pier.

On Saturday afternoon there was a Singaround session in the Foyer Hall compèred by Stuart Reed and in the same hall on Sunday afternoon a Sussex traditional concert featuring local favourites Eddie Upton, and Bob Lewis together with The Coppers, George Spicer, Bob Blake, Cyril Phillips, George Belton and Johnny Doughty. Also on Sunday afternoon, in the Main hall, there was a Ceilidh featuring the Pump and Pluck Band.

There was however little publicity and no liaison with the local club organisers. Fred totally ignored the fact that there was a thriving local scene with clubs meeting on Friday, Saturday and Sunday. This, in addition to the fact that it was a brand new venue and comparatively unknown not only to the folk enthusiasts but also to the public in general, was a recipe for disaster.

Jim Marshall had some unofficial advance notice through his contact with the manager of the Brighton Centre and rather belatedly an advertisement for the event was placed in the September-October issue of the Sussex Folk Diary, but the first official approach was a letter from Fred Woods asking if the clubs could provide people to steward the event, showing them to their seats and where the toilets were. Needless to say he received a rather short and to the point rejection.

As he recalls, Jim Marshall visited the centre for the opening night which featured Mike Harding with support from the Ian Campbell Folk Group, Joanna Carlin, Peter Bellamy, Dave Qualey from America and The Clutha with Gordeanna McCulloch. Only minutes before the show was due to start there were well under one hundred people in an arena with 3,000 seats. Jim didn't stay for the evening, preferring instead to go to Friday's Folk where the guests John Tams and the Excelsior Band proved more attractive to the local fans and drew a larger audience than the festival event.

The Saturday evening concert featured Five Hand Reel with support from Harvey Andrews, The Copper Family, Peter Bond, English Tapestry and Scheepsbeschuit from Holland.

Stuart Reed remembers the Sunday afternoon Sussex singers session being reasonably well attended but the evening concert featuring Burl Ives, with support from Therapy, Robin Hall and Jimmie MacGregor, Jean Redpath, Bill Caddick and Na Fili, being only about one third full.

Unsurprisingly there has not been another attempt to organise a major weekend festival in the area.

Firle Folk Day

Following the demise of the Lewes Folk Days, and after a lapse of three years, George Wagstaff, supported by the regulars of the music and song sessions at the Ram Inn, set out to organise a similar event in the village of Firle.

The Firle Folk Day was sponsored by the Ram Inn and Wealden Folk Project, under the guidance of Shirley Collins and funded by South East Arts.

Firle Folk day poster 1992 *the author*

Folk ▪ Firle

Saturday 5th September 1992

Events from 12 noon until 11pm.

Guests booked for your amazement, edification, amusement and divertion, are as follows:

The Olde -Worlde Charm of
The Copper Family

The Smiling and Dextrous
Mr. Ron Spicer

The Sweet Notes of
Miss Marilyn Bennett

The Ever Joyous Sounds of
Sussex Harmony

The Omni - Talented
Mr. Will Duke

The Ever Sprightly
Ditchling Morris

The Redoubtable
Mr. Gordon Hall

The Almost Thespian
Merrie England Mummers

The Stalwart
Mr. Bob Lewis

The Jovial and Rhythmic
Dan Quinntet

Plus, a special feature : 'Kipling's Sussex', a tribute to Peter Bellamy in words and music.

There will be dancing and music sessions throughout the day.

A special dance in the village hall will take place between 7pm and 9pm.

A concert will take place between 9pm and 11pm.

An extraordinary time is guaranteed for all!

Fully detailed Programme/Ticket £5. Further details are available only from :
Folk in Firle, Downside Cottage,
Peacehaven, Sussex BN10 7UB

The first event was on 1 September 1990 and based on two main venues, the village Memorial hall and the Ram Inn with an afternoon special 'Shepherds Diary' featuring the Copper family in St Peters Church. The Ram held a lunch time music session, a late afternoon Morris display and performance of the Firle Mummers play by the Merrie England Mummers and a harvest supper during the evening. Meanwhile the Memorial hall featured a craft fair and children's events during the afternoon and a dance in the evening. There were similar events on the first Saturday of September in 1991 [7th], 1992 [5th], 1993 [4th] and 1995 [3rd].

Initially George experienced local opposition to the event from residents who were distressed by their small village being 'taken over' for the day and all the extra cars parked along the roadsides, but careful negotiations resolved these concerns.

By 1995 however more obstacles arose, this time from South East Arts who were concerned at the 'loose' contracts that were used in the folk world. They wanted clear statements about items such as who was responsible for providing instruments and cover against possible non-appearance by a performer. Faced with what he considered too much 'red tape' George abandoned the project.

With the closure of yet another popular event Jerry Jordan responded to suggestions from a number of local performers and on 20 January 1996 initiated the Sussex Singaround, a daylong song session solely in the Ram at Firle.

This also was to prove an extremely popular event and became a regular feature of the Sussex folk calendar on the third Saturday of each January.

After four years Jerry decided to take a break from the organising and the first session of the new millennium in January 2000 was organised by the residents of the Lewes Arms Folk Club.

Jerry Jordan
Jim Marshall
and
Sussex Singaround poster 1999
the author

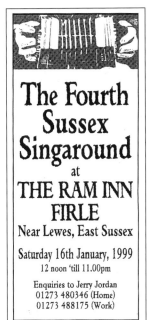

The Fourth Sussex Singaround
at
THE RAM INN FIRLE
Near Lewes, East Sussex

Saturday 16th January, 1999
12 noon 'till 11.00pm

Enquiries to Jerry Jordan
01273 480346 (Home)
01273 488175 (Work)

ENGLISH FOLK DANCE AND SONG SOCIETY [E.F.D.S.S.]

Many in the folk song world viewed the EFDSS as an irrelevance to the song revival but the apparent low profile of The Society, although possibly true for the organisation of folk song clubs nation wide, was not an accurate reflection of its general input to the awakening interest in folk song.

This was particularly true in Sussex where among local enthusiasts a number were not only active but also influential members of The Society, despite the fact that most had tended to join after they became interested in folk song because the Society was an umbrella organisation for their interest not because the Society had introduced them to the genre. Paul Setford was chairperson of the Sussex District Committee. Eddie Upton and I were, at various times, both members of the Sussex District Committee and also served on the Society's National Executive and various sub committees. Tony Wales was in a different position, he was employed by the Society as a full time staff member responsible for publicity, sales and editing the magazine when he formed the Horsham Songswappers and staged the first Horsham Festivals. Both Derek Lockwood, musician and one time Squire of Chanctonbury Ring Morris Men and Harry Mousdell, a long time Morris Dancer were, in addition to their singing, actively involved in organising folk activities in the county. Perhaps the most notable of all local performers associated with the E.F.D.S.S. was Doctor Vic Gammon, singer, instrumentalist, composer, lecturer, historian and writer. He obtained a doctorate in History at Sussex University in 1985 with his thesis, 'Popular Music in Rural Society: Sussex 1815-1914' and, apart from serving on the national Executive, became a member of the Editorial Board of the Society's Folk Music Journal in 1984, a position he still holds today.

Vic, a club resident at the Laughing Fish, Isfield and co-founder of the monthly music sessions at the Ram, Firle, was a frequent and popular performer both as guest and floor singer at all the clubs in and around Brighton. In addition he featured in several major folk groups and in the Mid Sussex Times on 26 January 1978 Vic Smith described the 'Pump and Pluck' band as the "hardest working folk group in the area" when he wrote *"When the Etchingham Steam Band decided to call it a day after two very successful years on the road, Vic Gammon thought he had had enough of the rigours of a travelling full time musician for a while and decided to work part-time with a band in and around Sussex while he went back to the University of Sussex to work on his thesis. He had played with an occasional band called the Pump and Pluck Band, and decided to put this on a more regular footing. The band has had quite a few changes in personnel during its life of nearly three years, but Will Duke, a founder member of the band is still there with Vic. Will is one of the musicians who augmented the Etchingham when they went to play at large dances or Ceilidhs, and then he played his anglo-concertina alongside Vic's melodeon and banjo. Ian Russell was also a founder member of the Pump and Pluck, but when he finished at Sussex University he was off to India for a year. Well, now he's back, living in London, and he has rejoined the band. He plays the banjo when the band are playing in folk clubs, but a sturdy trombone accompaniment below the tune when the band are playing for dances. Sheila Gammon plays the bass concertina – she and Vic were married earlier this month – and Pam Gilder comes along to sing with the band when they are in folk clubs. The dual role the Pump and Pluck Band play as a dance band and a folk club attraction makes them the hardest working folk group in our area."*

As Vic Smith also noted in the Mid Sussex paper later that year on 22 June Vic Gammon also featured in another popular Sussex group Potters Wheel. *"Terry Potter"*, a stalwart of the original Horsham Songswappers club, *"and his cousin Ian Holder, have been playing music together virtually all their lives in various bands. Including a successful time playing fully professional as part of the Etchingham Steam Band, ..."*

Returning to the E.F.D.S.S., the Society was involved with the promotion of folk song at an early stage of the local development providing support for the first Folk Festivals mentioned earlier at the Co-op and Ralli Halls in 1966, 67 and 68 It was also responsible for two major annual events that included folk song. The Sing and Play evenings at The New Inn, Hurstpierpoint and the Sussex Folk Night at Michelham Priory.

Hurstpierpoint Sing and Play sessions

These were Sunday evening events, which started on 11 February 1962 at the New Inn, Hurstpierpoint and then repeated, on an annual basis, for the next two years on 10 Feb 1963 and 9 Feb 1964. There is some confusion about who was the prime mover in the organisation of this event but regular performers and compères were Dick Playll and Jim Hoare from Shoreham who were members of both the Shoreham Folk Dance Club and Chanctonbury Ring Morris Men, Harry Mousdell from Horsham Songswappers, Don Lewry, sometime Chairman of Sussex District Committee of the E.F.D.S.S. and Derek Lockwood.

Derek Lockwood *Jim Marshall*

There were no guests but the session had a compère for the evening and then, rather like the Horsham Song-swappers, the invitation to entertain moved round the room with individuals or groups performing, either music, song or a Morris dance. They attracted singers and dancers, particularly Morris men from all over Sussex and in 1965 as interest in folk and support for the event increased so the number of sessions held each year doubled, meeting every six months. That year the early meeting was slightly later, on 25 April, but repeated after six months on 31 October and this pattern was repeated in 1966 on Sunday 1 May with Harry Mousdell and Derek Lockwood as compères.

Later, on Sunday 24 July 1966, it became an independent club with meetings monthly on the third Sunday, organised and hosted by Derek Lockwood and Clare Clayton. These sessions continued on that basis up to 16 February 1969.

Michelham Priory Folk Nights 1969-83

The Society had for some time organised two annual events, one in East and the other in West Sussex at Glynde and Arundel Castle respectively. These were dance evenings but in 1969 Derek Lockwood suggested something larger and more broad based. The Society's District Committee was wary of the idea and unsure if it would be a viable enterprise. Derek, along with Clare Clayton, were more certain and offered to underwrite the event with the Sing and Play evenings at Hurstpierpoint and so it was that on Saturday 31 May 1969 the Sussex District Committee of the EFDSS inaugurated a folk night at the moated Michelham Priory near Eastbourne. Outdoors, whilst daylight lasted, and then in the Great Barn there was dancing to The Ranchers with Francis Hawkins as MC. There were Morris dance displays by Chanctonbury Ring and Sussex University Morris Men and in a marquee a Songspot featuring Shirley Collins as guest with me as compère.

The format was repeated on 5 September the following year with Tim Hart and Maddy Prior and Miles Wootton at the songspot. Next year, 1971, the event moved to 5 June and was to remain an annual June event until 1983. The Ranchers remained the Saturday evening dance band until 1977 and returned in 1979. In 1976 a Friday evening dance was introduced and remained part of the event for the next three years when a Friday evening song concert was also introduced. 1980 was a barn Dance only and for the next three years there was a dance and songspot.

The song guest list over the life of the event was impressive. In 1971 it featured Martyn Wyndham-Read and Nic Jones with Miles Wootton as compère. For 18 June 1972 Cyril Tawney was guest with Miles Wootton and Bryan Blanchard as co-compères and in 1973 on 16 June, Dave Burland, again with Miles Wootton and Bryan Blanchard as hosts. On 15 June 1974 Gwyllam Wake, Pete and Christine Coe, Isobel Sutherland and Bryan Blanchard were featured and the following year, on 14 June 1975, Bob Davenport, Terry Masterson, and Chris Foster were the guests with Eddie Upton and Roger Brasier as co-hosts. Cyril Tawney made a return visit along with The Blackpool Taverners in 1976 on 19 June and in 1977, on the weekend of 24/25 June, there was a songspot with Alan White on Friday evening and Tony Capstick on Saturday. Two concerts were the feature in 1978, on 23 and 24 June. On Friday evening the guests were The Ratcliffe Stout Band and Mel Davies and on Saturday the second concert presented the [Brighton] Taverners, Eric Ilott and Folk Packet. In 1979 – 22/23 June – there was a Friday folk show featuring Martyn Wyndham-Read while the Saturday show presented Ticklers Jam, Packie Byrne and Bonnie Shaljean. The 1981 event, on 27 June, presented folk song by Tundra and in 1982 Spredthick were featured on 26 June. The final year, 25 June 1983 staged Anne Lennox-Martin and Sam Stephens.

7   KEY INDIVIDUALS
THE ORGANISERS

When looking at the history of the folk song clubs around the Brighton area including Worthing, Eastbourne and Lewes, among the many personalities involved there are a small number of committed individuals whose names recur again and again. They were and are the backbone of the song revival in the area, not necessarily as singers but as the club organisers. Without them the folk revival in Sussex could have been very different. One thing they all understood was that folk was not a commercial enterprise. Whatever their original motive might have been they, like all who organised a folk club, soon learnt that there was no money to be made, just a love of the music and pleasure at sharing it with others.

As Jim Marshall wrote in the Brighton and Hove Gazette Show Guide 'Folk Scene' on 16 September 1972:

"Running a folk club is a chancy business. It's almost impossible to guarantee a good evening. I've known occasions when a nationally-known guest has failed to attract the hoped-for large audience and others when a club with no guest booked has been packed to overflowing.

Such is the apparent fickleness of the folk club audience."

As early as 25 August 1967 Jim again in the Brighton and Hove Gazette Show Guide wrote:

"It amazes me when I see the occasional person walk up to the cash desk of one of the local clubs and then walk away muttering that the admission fee is too high." [At that time it would have been about 3 shillings or 15 pence.] *No one could honestly call the charges excessive. In fact, I would hazard a guess that no where else in Brighton can you get the same standard of entertainment for such a low cost.*

It must be that some people just don't realise the enormous expense involved in running a folk club, or a club of any kind for that matter. Gone are the days when a guest singer would come along for a couple of quid. Now they are nearly all in the hands of agency tycoons and fees have rocketed sky-high over the past few years. Admission charges on the other hand, have stayed more of less stationary. It has to be an exceptional evening for a club to make any profit at all and there are many occasions when the club funds take a steep dive. Besides having to pay high fees to the guests, there is also the hire of the room, advertising, printing costs and, if they can afford it payment to the resident singers. It's really the resident singers who carry the club and, more often than not, they give their services for no reward."

Things change quickly and not always for the better. Just four months later on 22 December in the same paper Jim wrote:

"Just when the clubs are in the midst of their Christmas and New Year festivities comes a hint that all will not be well on the folk scene in 1968. The shadow that is looming is that of higher fees to performers. This week I received from one of the biggest folk agencies in the country a list of singers on their books together with the cost of engaging these singers for a folk club. Whereas a few years ago one could secure the services of a competent performer for six or eight pounds they are now asking as much as £100 for a solo singer. One well-known female artist, much loved by the TV masses, is asking, and very often getting, £400 for an hour's singing."

With this is mind it seems appropriate to record some of the longer serving club organisers, their background and how they acquired their love of folk music.

Jim Marshall

Pre-eminent among local enthusiasts, Jim was one of the few club organisers who was not also a performer and in some ways this makes his dedication to the folk song movement for 36 years quite remarkable.

His interest in the folk scene 'evolved' from the popular music of his youth which had a slightly American country style through an interest in jazz, when he remembers attending a concert in Nottingham featuring Sonny Terry and

Brownie McGhee, to the present day enthusiasm for both folk and country music.

Jim Marshall *Jim Marshall*

He was one of the first members of the original Ballads and Blues club when it opened on 24 September 1961 and was an early supporter of Johnie Winch's club first at The Heart In Hand and then at The Stanford Arms.

In 1965 he was co-founder of the first Brighton Country and Western club and in 1966, following the departure of Johnie Winch, became co-organiser of the Brighton Singers Club. Eventually becoming sole organiser, a role he was to carry out for the next 21 years until it finally closed as Berties Folk Night at The Prince Albert on 1 February 1987. By then it was a nationally renowned club due largely to the efforts of Jim.

He quickly returned to club organisation with sessions at first The Stanford Arms and then The Springfield from April 1987 to June 1992. His next venture was outside Brighton when, together with Vic and Tina Smith, he was involved with organising The Royal Oak Folk Club, Lewes from April 1993 to 1997.

His contribution to publicising folk song is possibly even greater. From 1969 to 1981 he was Folk Correspondent with the Brighton and Hove Gazette writing weekly articles on both the local clubs and the national scene. From 1968 until 1970 he produced a monthly programme of folk for BBC Radio Brighton and from 1971 through until 1996 he, together with Vic Smith, produced the longest running folk programme on British radio the weekly Minstrels Gallery for the local station BBC Radio Sussex.

'FOLK' from the Brighton and Hove Gazette 3 Dec 1971

"Radio series is going well.

MONDAY sees the seventh programme in the new Minstrels' Gallery series on Radio Brighton. Initial reaction to the first half dozen shows has been very good and, looking at the list of people lined up for future appearances, I am certain it is going to build up quite a large regular audience.

Already there are reports from people who have heard the efforts of other local stations that Brighton's folk programme is among the best, which is quite encouraging.

This week's edition brings to the studio Tony Rose who will be talking about his newest LP and playing a track or two from it plus, of course, a local singer and there will be the usual record review and a run-down on the local folk news.

You can hear Minstrels' Gallery this coming Monday at 6.30 p.m.

Actually, one of the first records to be reviewed on the new programme was The Wide Midlands the anthology of songs from around Birmingham which Topic records released a short time back. Among the many singers on the album were Christine Richards and Pete Coe and they will be down here in Brighton this evening as guests of the SPRINGFIELD HOTEL folk club.

As you would expect their songs are traditional, but they have recently been writing some of their own material although still in the vernacular vein.

At the LEWES ARMS in Lewes tomorrow night Ron Simmonds will be appearing in place of scheduled Terry Masterson. Terry is still in Canada but I am he sure would approve of his replacement, for both he and Ron shared for a long time the residency at London's only seven-day-a-week rendezvous, Bunjies Coffee bar.

Although I missed it I am told that Ron's most recent visit to the Lewes club was outstanding, so a repetition is on the cards for tomorrow.

Next February sees the release of the second album for United Artists by Brighton's Allan Taylor. It has already been recorded and will contain mainly songs of his own writing plus an odd traditional ballad. On Sunday he is back at the STANFORD ARMS club on Preston Circus, the club which was his home for so long.

Sunday is also the day for the monthly Guitar at the MARLBOROUGH club in Princes Street, Brighton. This month its guests are brother and sister flamenco guitar duetists, Adrian and Yvonne Lynch, plus local Spanish dancer Teresa, who will be accompanied by the club's resident Mike Trory. Sounds like quite a fiesta!

Another Sunday club, which is usually outside the area I cover, is that at Eastbourne and, as many Brighton people visit it from time to time I had better mention that it has closed its doors until the spring. I will let you know when it reopens.

Tuesday night's the regular date for the Taverners' session at the ARLINGTON on Marine Parade and on the same evening there is another of the highly popular Lazy River Hoedowns at the HUNTINGDON HALL, Buckingham Road, Shoreham. It starts at 8.15 p.m. and goes on until 10.30.

From all accounts the most popular group ever to play at the RICHMOND Country and Western Club have been Pinkerton County. They visited the club in its early days and returned only recently to deputise for another outfit which cancelled at the last minute.

They obviously generated a great deal of enthusiasm, so much so that they are back for the third time this coming Thursday. Another singer soon to make a return to this club is Little Ginny, but more of that next week.
Jim Marshall"

In 1969 he was co-founder and editor of The Brighton Folk Diary which evolved first into The Sussex Folk Diary and then simply The Folk Diary. This popular guide to what's on around the local clubs is still running today [2002] after 32 years and still with Jim as co-editor.

In addition to his local activities Jim has gained a national and international reputation for his knowledge of Country Music. He was, in 1968, a founder member of the British Country Music Association and within five years became Chairman of the Association, a role he still holds today after 28 years. In addition he edits an informative bi-monthly Country Music newsletter and is involved with organising the Association's annual trip to the United States of America. If this was not enough he was, from August 1990, presenter of "That's Country" on BBC Radio Sussex.

On 20 June 1996 at the Royal Oak club in Lewes, with Brian Golbey – one of the early residents from the Stanford Arms club and co-founder of the first Brighton Country Club – as guest, the local folk fraternity made a presentation to Jim in recognition of his 30 years of unbiased involvement in all aspects of the local folk scene. Clearly a mark of the high esteem in which he is held by his contemporaries.

Jim was not however a native of Brighton, not even of Sussex. He was born in 1935 in Sutton in Ashfield, Nottinghamshire where his father was a teacher and his grandfathers were, respectively, a publican and a watch repairer.

After attending the Grammar School in Mansfield he served National Service in the Royal Air Force and worked briefly on the railway before his family moved to Brighton in 1959 when his father secured a post in the town. His uncle was already a Brighton resident as landlord of The Stanford Arms, a position that was eventually to prove a very happy relationship when the need arose for the Brighton Blues and Gospel club to seek another venue from the Heart In Hand. Virtually all of Jim's working life until he accepted early retirement in 1990 was spent as an administrator with Bush Signs.

Jim Marshall 1996 Presentation of 30 years award by friends.
Jerry Jordan [*standing left*]**, Bill Evans** [*standing centre*]**, an early regular at the Sunday Folk Club and one time organiser of a monthly session at the Gun in Findon and Brian Golbey** [*seated right*] *Jim Marshall*

Tina and Vic Smith

Tina and Vic's involvement in the Sussex folk scene started a little later but was to be long and significant. They are still actively involved today after 34 years.

Their first club was at The Gloucester in December 1968, moving in July 1969 to The Prince George and to The Marlborough in 1970 where it closed in April. Next, in March 1970 following Jack Whyte's departure for Canada, Terry Masterson enlisted Vic and Tina as co-residents at The Pug O' Junch folk club in Lewes and in 1973 they took over the running of the club from Terry.

In 1974 the club was renamed The Lewes Arms Folk Club and in 1978 it transferred to The Royal Oak where it closed briefly in February 1979. In July 1979 it reopened at The Brewers Arms and in 1982 transferred to The Laughing Fish at Isfield where Vic and Tina, after 15 years in charge, finally left in August 1988.

From 1969 to 1974 they were involved in running the Co-op Folk Days in the grounds of the Royal Pavilion, Brighton and then from 1974 to 1987 with two breaks – 1983 and 1985 – they were responsible for organising the hugely popular Lewes Folk Day.

These two stalwarts of the local scene returned to club organising in April 1993 in a joint venture with Jim Marshall at The Royal Oak Folk Club, Lewes which is still running today.

Tina and Vic Smith
Terry Masterson

As with Jim Marshall, Tina and Vic's contribution to the Sussex folk scene went far beyond running clubs. They too became deeply involved in publicising folk song to a wider audience. In 1969 they were co-founders and Editors, along with Jim Marshall, of The Brighton Folk Diary, now after 32 years running simply as The Folk Diary but still with Vic as co-editor. From 1971 through until 1996 Vic and initially Tina, together again with Jim Marshall, produced the weekly Minstrels Gallery for BBC local radio

Following Jim's example Vic also entered local journalism becoming folk correspondent to the Brighton and Hove Herald from 1969 to 1972, the Mid Sussex Times from 1972 to 1981 and then, from 1981 to 1988, he and Tina wrote articles alternate weeks for the Sussex Express.

Tina [Christine] née Ball was born in Portsmouth, Hampshire in 1945 where the family life had strong musical influences. Her mother played the piano, her father sang and her sister played trumpet in the style of Harry James. As a consequence the house was full of music.

The first time she heard live folk music was in the Railway Inn folk club in Portsmouth, although she usually went to the jazz club, which was where she first met Vic.

After leaving school she attended teacher-training college in London just round the corner from where Vic was then living. She started visiting Vic's college folk club and other folk venues in the area and gradually started singing, accompanying herself on an anglo-concertina, which she had bought.

In 1966 she married Vic and together they ran folk clubs in Woolwich and Blackheath. In the early days she was strongly influenced by the many visits made to Scottish festivals notably Blairgowrie and later Kinross, but as she became more familiar with the music she gravitated towards Irish and English music and songs.

Tina Smith *Tina and Vic Smith*

After two years, in 1968, they moved to Brighton when Tina decided on a career change and qualified as a librarian at what was then the Brighton Polytechnic, now the Brighton College of Technology. She found an English concertina in a junk shop soon after moving to Brighton and with Lea Nicholson as inspiration and teacher was soon playing it at the Gloucester club which she and Vic opened in December 1968. They moved to Lewes in 1978 and she now works at the Learning Resource Centre of Lewes Tertiary College.

Tina is deeply involved behind the scenes in organising their club at the Royal Oak while publicly she sings and plays the concertina. Away from the song club she has been in two concertina bands – Nigel Chippindale's 'Creepy Crawley Concertina Combo' and 'The Dodgy Button Band. She has played in several barn dance bands including 'The Lewes Band' and 'Four Piece Suite'. Her current band is the popular 'Sussex Pistols' formed in 1992.

Vic Smith was born in Edinburgh in 1943 but was educated in Portsmouth where his father, who was in the navy, was stationed. Although his parents were not musical his uncle was, being a fiddle player with his own Scottish dance band and it was this type of music and the Jimmy Shand band that were among his early subconscious influences. A more direct influence was the BBC "Tonight" programme which regularly featured folk singers Robin Hall and Jimmie MacGregor, Cy Grant, and the McEwen brothers, Alex and Rory. His introduction to live folk music came in Portsmouth during the early 1960's when he visited the famous Railway Folk Club, which met at the pub he normally visited to listen to jazz.

Moving to London, initially to work in the Purchasing Section of Boots, he then attended college and trained as teacher. In London he again met Christine [Tina] Ball and as noted earlier they married in 1966. On completion of his training Vic secured a post in Lancing before they moved to Brighton in September 1968 He now teaches at a Special Needs school in Seaford. While in London he was co-resident and organiser of two folk clubs but his introduction to the local folk scene came within a month of moving to Brighton when he attended the Sussex Folk Festival held in the Ralli Hall at Hove and the rest is, as they say history.

Vic Smith *Tina and Vic Smith*

Apart from his involvement with folk song in the Brighton area as performer, broadcaster, magazine editor and event organiser Vic is an experienced dance band musician and caller, working for the past eight years with the busy 'Sussex Pistols' band.

He is also a folk journalist, currently writing for a range of folk and traditional music publications including 'Musical Traditions' and 'Folk Roots'.

Terry Masterson

Terry's history as a club organiser is not as long as those already mentioned, spanning the periods from 1964 to 1971, 1982 to 1983 and 1990. It was however extremely significant in that he was involved with the creation of two of the longest running clubs in the area, first in Brighton and then Lewes. His involvement as a resident singer is however much longer and he remains today after 38 years a firm favourite as a guest singer at all the local clubs.

Terry arrived in Brighton at the invitation of Jack Whyte, to join him as resident at the Friday Folk Club which they opened on 6 March 1964. When Jack left for Canada in 1967 Terry took over the organisation until handing that over to Paul Setford in September 1969.

His next involvement was again with Jack, this time in Lewes where they opened The Pug O' Junch club at The Lewes Arms in March 1965. As with the Brighton Friday club when Jack left for Canada Terry assumed the mantle of club organiser, asking Vic and Tina Smith to join him as residents in 1969 before handing the organisation over to them in 1971.

He was also involved with Jack again and Miles Wootton in organising Worthing's second folk club at The Malsters in March 1966, although this club only survived for a year, and running the Home Spun concert at the Dome in November 1966.

After spending a year [1971/2] in the USA touring colleges and singing Terry returned to Brighton and in the 1980's was again resident along with Vic and Tina when they moved the Lewes Folk club [as the Pug O' Junch was then called] out to The Laughing Fish at Isfield.

Terry Masterson *Jim Marshall*

His last venture as an organiser of a formal club was from April 1982 to July 1983 on Wednesday evenings at The Royal Oak, St James Street Brighton, initially with Chris Littledale and Mike McRory-Wilson and briefly, until his health deteriorated, Keith Johns. He was also involved as resident and host of a session at the Elephant and Castle in Lewes during the summer of 1990.

Terry was born in 1935 in Bedford where his father, who came from Ireland, was a commercial traveller. When his family moved to London he was educated at St Michael's College, a Catholic boarding school in Hitchin, Hertfordshire and after leaving school spent two years National Service in The Royal Enniskillen Fusiliers based initially in Omagh and then in Kenya. Returning to civilian life he rejoined his family in Twickenham and was quickly attracted by the creative arts and joined the local Art College as a mature student. Soon after leaving there he had two 'One Man' Exhibitions in Richmond first at the local Theatre and then the art gallery. To supplement his career as an artist he worked for a while on the Continental Telephone Exchange as a linguist and then started singing in Bunjies Coffee Bar in London. It was from here that Jack Whyte, whom he had met earlier in Twickenham when he was a resident at the Crown Folk Club, persuaded him to move to Brighton to join in setting up the Friday's Folk Club.

Like so many of the early converts to the folk scene his first contact was in the 50's when he bought a guitar and formed a skiffle group which played in pubs and other venues on the outskirts of West London. His experience of this type of music had however started at a much younger age. He grew up with a folk background in which his father would tell him innumerable Irish folk tales whilst visits to his grandfather and uncles who lived in and around Baldoyle, just outside Dublin, always meant evenings of music and song in the traditional Irish style. Apart from the family connection with music making, his National Service stint in the army was also an important influence musically and many of the songs in his repertoire were acquired at this time. Even after he became involved with skiffle he continued singing in a more traditional style among friends and families within the Irish community. As Terry recalls "I cannot remember a time when I was not interested in the 'Ould Songs', and when I could obtain the words I would sing them at parties and such like gatherings. I suspect that this was regarded as a little eccentric by my schoolfellows who were only interested in the more orthodox kinds of popular music. My début in the world of Folk Music was in 1958 when, as a very nervous singer from the floor, I stood up in a Twickenham club held on Eel Pie Island in the middle of the Thames. It was run by American singer Sandy Paton and presented all the top names of the day, such as Jack Elliott, Robin Hall, Dominic Behan and even a skiffle group with a young Leon Rosselson." He was surprised to find there were clubs around catering for his type of music but it was just what he was looking for. "My repertoire in those days consisted of Irish and Scottish songs only, but it has since expanded to include English, American and West Indian material." Later on he met another singer, Theo Johnson, who asked him to help in a folk lecture. This led to Terry being asked to become a resident at Bunjies, one of London's better known rendezvous, and also joining the Twickenham club as a resident. He left the latter shortly before moving to Brighton but continued at Bunjies for some time after. His trip to the United States and Canada in 1971 also resulted in him teaming up with his old friend Jack Whyte, by then a professional singer, and together under the name 'The Heather Heathens' touring Western Canada playing mostly bars and hotels. Despite this lifetime of involvement with singing he claims to still suffer from 'butterflies' before a performance but has learnt 'to live with it'. This was not so at his inauspicious début as a guest singer many years ago at a club onboard a barge moored on The Thames at Kew when he took a drop or two to steady his nerves before going on and ended up collapsing in mid song.

Paul Setford

Paul Setford, unlike most of the long term club organisers in and around Brighton, was actually born in the county at Haywards Heath in 1941. He also differed from the other organisers in that he did not actually found a club, nevertheless his commitment to folk activities was long and very important covering a span of 40 years.

He first became interested in folk songs in the late 1950's when his early inspirations were Burl Ives, Pete Seeger and later, Cyril Tawney. Inspired by Pete Seeger, whom he heard in concert at the Ralli Hall, Hove he made his début performance shortly afterwards as a floor singer at the Brighton Ballads and Blues Club in the Hideout Ballroom, East Street during the autumn of 1961.

Development was steady and he became a regular floor singer at many of the local clubs leading, in 1964, to a residency at the Shoreham folk. In 1969 he succeeded Terry Masterson as organiser and resident of the Brighton Friday's Folk Club at The Springfield where he remained until 1980 before 'retiring' due to other commitments. Although only five years old the club was, nevertheless, well established when Paul took it over but by the time he handed it over to Eddie Upton it was into its sixteenth year and recognised as not only one of Brighton's, but also the country's, major folk venues. A popular singer with a repertoire of mainly British traditional songs he was, during his time at Friday's Folk, a regular broadcaster on Radio Brighton's' Minstrel Gallery. In 1969 he was, along with Jim Marshall and Vic Smith, one of the three club organisers responsible for the creation of the Brighton Folk Diary.

Paul Setford
Jim Marshall

Paul's enthusiasm for the folk tradition however pre-dates his interest in singing and he has spent much of his life in various folk activities. He was an active member of the Worthing Grasshoppers folk dance club from 1958 to 1964 but of much more significance was his membership of the Chanctonbury Ring Morris club. Not just a keen but also fine dancer he joined Chanctonbury Ring Morris Men in 1960, was squire from 1963 to 1965 and Dance Captain, teaching all the new men and new dances to the club, for over thirty years from 1963 to 1996 – apart for a short break of three years in the mid 1980's.

An active member of the English Folk Dance and Song Society [EFDSS] he was chairperson of both the Sussex District Committee and South East Area Council and in addition represented the South East Area on the National Executive Committee for three years from 1973 to 1975.

Paul's long term commitment to song and dance was rewarded in 1994 when he received the 'Scan Tester Award' given annually by the Sussex District of the EFDSS in recognition of services to folk in the county.

Born in Haywards Heath he moved to Worthing within a few months when his father, who worked for the Post Office telecommunications section, transferred to the coast. It was there that Paul grew up, attending the Worthing

High School for Boys. After leaving school Paul joined the Civil Service in 1959 and has spent his entire working life with the Inland Revenue at Durrington in West Sussex. Since his marriage he has lived in near-by Goring by Sea.

Paul's family was long time residents of Horsted Keynes, where his father was born, and were for generations friends of the Tester family. His grandfather, who at different times had various occupations including foreman of a local brickyard and running the village shop, was a friend of Tranter Tester [Scan's brother] while his great grandfather was a farmer and brickyard owner.

Fred Baxter

Fred Baxter was an enigma, a complex individualist he was outwardly extrovert but also quiet and thoughtful. He was born in Southport, Lancashire in 1930 where his father was a joiner. Fred joined the army as a regular soldier at the age of eighteen and served with the R.A.S.C. for eight years during which he spent some time attached to the Supreme Headquarters Allied Powers Europe [SHAPE] at Fontainebleau, France and in 1951 whilst stationed in Newton Abbott met and married a local girl although they were subsequently divorced in 1972.

After being discharged from the army on medical grounds in 1955 he had a variety of jobs in the south west and Wales before arriving in Lewes in 1970, courtesy of Her Majesty's Government, when he was released from Lewes prison after a conviction for breaking and entering [Cat burglary as he described it]. He was given a home and a sense of belonging by Molly Gilbert, a political activist, and lodged with her until her death in 1994. After that Fred eventually moved into sheltered accommodation in Peacehaven and then on to a flat in Seaford. After a series of admissions to hospitals he was moved to a nursing home in Exeter near his eldest daughter where he died in 1998 at the age of sixty-seven.

Fred Baxter
Mrs R J Harvey
[formerly Mrs Baxter]

158

With Molly he was active in local political circles becoming at various times both Secretary and Vice Chairperson of the Lewes Branch of the Labour Party he was also an ardent supporter of the Campaign for Nuclear Disarmament [CND] and concerned with animal rights. He was genial, gregarious and a well known character to most people in the town and again with Molly active in the Westgate Chapel organisation where he had a carpentry workshop and also, from time to time, acted as host for its One World Centre. He joined the Lewes Little Theatre Company and was a talented amateur actor although he was always willing to help out with any backstage activity.

As his ex-wife recalls, Fred was always singing, mostly folk and old songs rather than tunes of the day. When he arrived in Lewes he was soon immersed in the local folk scene first as a singer, where he displayed an extensive repertoire including many music hall items and anti war or protest songs, then as a club organiser. His first formal folk club was 'Folk at the Elephant' which he opened in the autumn of 1977 but this closed after six months.

Soon after opening the Elephant in 1977 Fred started informal singarounds at the Black Horse, these were undeniably his forte, initially a Sunday lunch time session which was hugely successful it soon expanded to twice a week with regular Tuesday evening meetings, both with Fred in the 'chair'. These lasted until 1981 when the landlord decided he needed the room to expand his catering trade and Fred transferred the Sunday lunch time session to the Royal Oak where it remained until 1986 when the brewery modernised the pub and 'retired' the landlady. During this time, from October 1978 until August 1979, Fred was also one of the resident singers at 'The Ox Folk Club' meeting on Thursday evenings at the Sussex Ox, Milton Street.

In 1982 Fred opened 'Folk in the Oak', another formal folk club, which met on Sunday evenings at the Royal Oak and ran with mixed fortunes until 1985. This was not however to be Fred's last folk activity for in the early winter of 1987 he restarted a Saturday evening folk club at the Lewes Arms and continued to be involved with its organisation until 1994 when Molly died.

In all Fred gave some 17 enthusiastic and continuous years' service to organising folk song in Lewes.

Sandra Goddard

Another 'import' to Sussex was Sandra Goddard [née Wilson]. Born in Cuffley, Hertfordshire in 1940 she was educated at St Albans Girls Grammar School and in 1958 immediately after leaving school came to Sussex to Brighton Training College where in 1960 she qualified as a teacher. Her first teaching post was back in Hertfordshire in St Albans for two years before transferring to a school in Luton in January 1963.

There she soon formed what was to be a life long friendship with fellow teacher Mary McGannon. Mary asked Sandra if she liked folk music, to which

159

she replied, in effect, "what's that?" "Come along to the club I run." said Mary, which she did and as Sandra describes it, she was immediately 'hooked'. Unsurprisingly, later that year when she decided to take a degree in English at Hull University it was not long before she was visiting the folk sessions in The Bluebell Inn in Lowgate which was the 'home' of the Watersons club. She soon became friendly with the family and recalls evenings baby-sitting and later hitch-hiking with Norma to visit Johnny Handle at the Black Gate Museum in Newcastle.

Graduating with an Honours degree in English Literature in 1966 she quickly decided that she wanted to return to Sussex to live and secured a post teaching at a local junior school. A dedicated teacher she is still working within that profession today, 36 years later.

Her first week back in town proved to be critical in her development. During the week she visited a folk session organised by Bob Morris in 'Jimmie's' in St James Street and from there was 'directed' to Friday's Folk at the Springfield. There, a few nights later, her first contact, as it was for virtually all visitors, was the Club's 'doorman' Laurie Goddard, mentioned earlier. Two years later in August 1968 they were married. In between however she had been persuaded to start singing and remembers her first floor spot at the club was in the autumn of 1967 when she sang 'Lord Franklin' and 'The barley and the rye'. She was soon a regular singer not only in Brighton but also at the Pug o' Junch in Lewes where she always enjoyed great support and encouragement from organiser Vic Smith, without which, she says, she probably would not have continued singing.

Sandra & Laurie Goddard
Jim Marshall

Her great love of traditional songs was not really surprising for although she grew up enjoying classical music, particularly string quartets, there was a family background of songs from the folk idiom. Her maternal grandfather was a Scottish miner from near Glasgow and sang songs by Burns while her paternal grandmother was from London's East End and sang the songs she learnt from frequent visits to the old music halls. Sandra's first involvement with folk was quite early when she was coerced into playing washboard in her younger brother's skiffle group – albeit in the garden shed.

After returning to Brighton in 1966 she was, for almost fifteen years, until it closed in 1983, one of the most regular floor singers at Friday's Folk in Brighton and also a popular and possibly the most ubiquitous floor singer at every other club in the area.

From 1978 to 1980 Sandra was co-resident, with Brian Ablett at the Ditchling Folk Night after which, from 1981 to 1983, she became co-organiser, again with Brian and then, when he stood down, the sole organiser of the regular monthly singarounds at the Thatched Inn, Keymer until 1988.

Briefly, for five months in the summer of 1988, after the return of Jim and Heather Keelty to the Springfield in Brighton she ran a song and tune session there.

A regular floor singer at the Lewes Arms folk club, Lewes, when it was re-opened by Fred Baxter in 1987 a year later in Dec 1988 she became a resident. Then, from December 1993 until the present time has been a key member of the committee that succeeded Fred as organisers of the club.

In 1992, starting on 15 September she founded another very popular monthly sing-around session, meeting on the third Tuesday of each month, in the Ram at Firle which she continues to organise now at the turn of the century. These sessions are designed to encourage new singers or to provide a forum for established performers to introduce new songs.

In all Sandra has given over thirty years' support to the local folk scene. First, for eleven years as a regular floor singer at most clubs in and around Brighton after which, for most of the next twenty-four years while continuing as a floor singer and occasional guest performer, she became organiser of a succession of highly popular and successful sing-around sessions and clubs.

The most recent addition to the list of long term organisers in the Brighton area is **Tim Kent**, a professional entertainer, who arrived in the city 17 years ago. He soon became immersed in the local folk scene and his first venture, opening on Tuesday 12 March 1985, was a singaround session 'Noblefolk' meeting weekly in Noble's Wine Bar, New Road, Brighton. After almost a year the sessions were transferred, first to the Queen's Head, Steine Street and shortly after to Nash's Hotel, Marine Parade. After a few months, in December 1986 there was a return to Noble's Wine Bar where the singarounds continued until September 1990 although the meetings changed to a Thursday evening and the premises were renamed Mrs Fitzherberts.

A month after closing these sessions Tim took over the organising of Folk in the Elephant in Lewes until February 1993 when he reverted to Brighton by opening Hanbury Folk at the Hanbury Arms in Kemp Town. This however was to be a relatively short-lived venture, closing at the end of December that year. Tim returned to club organising with the Wizard Folk Club meeting in the Prince Albert, Trafalgar Street on Tuesday evenings from April 1995 until January 1996 and then, four years later on 5 December 2000 he, together with John Collyer, opened the monthly 'Folk/Blues and Beyond' sessions in the Schooner Inn, Southwick which are still running today.

Tim Kent at BBC Radio Sussex *Tim Kent*

In addition to his club organising Tim was a member of the production team for the BBC local radio's Minstrels' Gallery for six years from 1989 and, more recently in 1999 formed his own recording company which has to date produced over thirty CD's of local singers and club sessions on his HAT label.

Tim was born in Marylebone, London in 1946 and became interested in the guitar during the skiffle era. His father played the piano but Tim's early musical influences were Lonnie Donegan, Bob Dylan Joan Baez and Donovan. Unlike so many of the local folk club organisers his family had property in Sussex and he spent a lot of time in his early youth in Angmering on Sea, West Sussex. During this time he was lead guitarist in a 'beat' group called The Scorpions which won a competition staged at the Odeon cinema, Littlehampton. His first 'folk' floor spot however was around 1967 in London at the Black Bull in Barnet and Whetstone. During the late 60's he was involved in organising small singaround sessions at pubs in Camden Town and Kensington and also ran a folk club at the London YMCA/YWCA.

It is interesting to reflect that only Jim Marshall of the long serving organisers was not a singer. Conversely of all the long serving resident singers only one was not also a long-term club organiser. The singer in question being:

Miles Wootton

Miles arrived in Brighton in 1965 but his interest in folksong began some years earlier. Born in 1934 in Manchester where his father, a professional musician, was playing violin in a BBC orchestra he also had a touch of show business in his veins since his mother was a former professional dancer with the world famous Tiller Girls. He moved to Worthing in 1942, when his father joined the Worthing Municipal Orchestra, and attended Worthing High School for Boys. At 18 he went up to Jesus College, Oxford and obtained a BA Degree in languages. Whilst there he visited the Oxford Union Folk Club and had his first encounter with the folk idiom.

After obtaining a teaching post in London he was sharing a flat with John Pole and through him met an aspiring drama student Mel Smith who subsequently moved in to their 'commune'. Together they formed a duo called unsurprisingly 'Mel and Miles' and performed in cabaret in London, Oxford and the Channel Islands. Then in 1964 they were offered a six-week summer residency at the Count House Club at Bottalack in Cornwall. Not knowing what would be required they arrived with a repertoire of mainly music hall ballads and cabaret songs only to find that it was a folk club. They quickly set about learning more folk material and at the end of the season returned to London where they ran a folk club in Hammersmith for about a year.

Miles Wootton *Jim Marshall*

After this Miles moved back to the Sussex coast and from 1966 to 1967 sang as a resident and co-organiser with Jack Whyte and Terry Masterson at the Troubadours, Worthing's second Folk Club. During 1967 Miles appeared at the Brighton Singers Club as one of the monthly residents following the departure of Brian Golbey and in the autumn teamed up for two years with Allan 'Spud' Taylor for what was a highly successful song-writing partnership with 'Spud' providing the music and Miles writing the lyrics. After 'Spud' left Miles continued as resident at the Sunday club for another eighteen years until 1987. During this time he was a frequent and popular guest artiste at all the local clubs and still performs today. Possibly his greatest contribution to the folk world however is the many songs he composed.

Vic Smith noted this in the Mid Sussex Times on 29 July 1976 when he wrote, *"The pitfalls facing the singer/songwriter in the folk club seem to be many. Some seem to write only to please themselves and often lose their way into introspection. Others seem to veer too much the other way – being so keen in trying to keep up with the latest trendy subjects that their songs all become part of the anonymous mish-mash of contemporary conversational clichés. Very few seem to be able to stamp distinguishing style on a number of songs so that you can say "Ah yes, that's a Jake Thackray song or a Jeremy Taylor song"– or whatever. When you get two like those I have mentioned it is possible for them to make quite a comfortable living for themselves from their singing. So it is quite surprising to find one of the songwriters whom many people consider to be one of the foremost in his style teaching in a school in Brighton and doing a bit of singing only in his spare time. Miles Wootton commands a lot of respect and his songs have been recorded by a large number of singers as different as Francoise Hardy, Fred Wedlock and the Fairport Convention. At long last there has recently become available an album of Miles singing his own songs. It's called "Sunday Supplement World" and it's on the Long Man label"*

There were of course other people who organised clubs in the area but their involvement was for comparatively short periods although two were particularly notable.

First **Johnie [also Johnny] Winch** who, although born in Horley in 1942, had moved to Brighton in 1952 after living for a while in South Africa. A former art student, he was already something of a local hero through his multi instrumental skills on both the guitar and banjo when folk 'arrived' in the town at informal folk sessions in the Ballad Tree coffee bar and the Eagle public house.

Johnie Winch *Jim Marshall*

Johnie was probably best known for gospel type songs and earned the name of "Reverend John Winch" through the audience participation that was a feature of the clubs at that time. He was also however a fine blues guitarist and singer whose repertoire included everything from American country to British traditional material.

Soon after the club scene started to develop he was responsible, between 1963 and 1966, for the evolution of the Sunday evening singarounds in the Heart in Hand into first the 'Country and Gospel' club and then 'Brighton Singers Club' at the Stanford Arms. This was to become one of the two major folk clubs in the town for the next twenty-six years.

After this he was involved with the early organisation of the first Eastbourne folk club at the Dolphin, again on Sunday evenings, until 1971. He eventually became a full time professional singer and moved out of the area, first to Hastings, then to Germany from where he worked extensively across the continent, then back to Hastings and finally back again to live in Germany.

Secondly, **Jack Whyte**, a teacher of English and drama born in Motherwell, Scotland who arrived in Brighton in the autumn of 1963.

Jack had sung from an early age, first as a boy soprano in the Cathedral choir of his hometown and then by the time he was 18 as the bass soloist in his Grammar School Choir. He discovered folk music whilst at College in London on a visit to a folk club in Twickenham and soon after that became a regular floor singer at a club in central London. It was at this time that he met Terry Masterson and together they briefly ran a club in Twickenham before Jack moved to Hove to take up his first teaching post.

Jack Whyte
Tom Groome [courtesy of Ron Pope]

In Sussex his superb voice soon gained him an invitation to join the residents at the first Shoreham folk club and two months later on 6 March 1964 he opened his own 'Friday's Folk' at the Springfield along with Terry Masterson. Never one to understate the situation Jack had written, in the early part of 1964, to Terry, then still in London, inviting him to join him in Sussex for a folk venture as "Brighton is wide open for folk music". Terry accepted and it is to Jack that the locals are indebted for the arrival in the town of the universally popular Terry. A year later on Saturday 6 March 1965 he, again with Terry, opened the Pug 'O Junch club in Lewes and then exactly one year later again on Sunday 6 March 1966, together with Terry and Miles Wootton, he opened 'The Troubadours' the second Worthing folk club.

Both the Brighton and Lewes ventures went on to become major long running clubs in the area while the Worthing club lasted only one year closing in 1967. In that summer, after four important years in the development of folk song in the Brighton area, Jack moved abroad to Canada initially as a teacher, then a full time professional singer and eventually as an author of Arthurian novels. One other significant effort was the realisation in 1966 of his dream of presenting a concert at The Dome featuring local artistes.

Before closing this chapter it is appropriate to mention one other local folk enthusiast, **Brian Matthews**.

Brian and Audrey Matthews
Brian Matthews

Brian was neither a club organiser, nor a regular singer around the folk clubs as they developed. In fact he had no long-term involvement with the Brighton scene. He did however, back in 1957, organise the first skiffle club in Brighton and later ran the Ballad Tree coffee bar. This was the first venue dedicated to providing a meeting place for folk enthusiasts and a place where they were able to sing, long before amateur live music became acceptable in public places. Even more significant perhaps was the fact that he had made the transition to traditional British folk music while other local performers were still performing Negro blues and American folk songs.

The field recordings he made on regular excursions into the Sussex countryside during the late 1950's, accompanied, a little reluctantly, by his wife Audrey, to listen to and gather material from the well known traditional performer George 'Pop' Maynard and lesser known singers such as George Townshend, Harry Holman, Jim Wilson, Jim 'Brick' Harber, Sarah Porter and Louie Saunders were put to good use in 2000/1 when Musical Traditions issued three CD's. One of George Townshend "Come Hand to Me the Glass" and a double set of North Sussex Traditional Singers "Just Another Saturday Night", all from the tapes recorded by Brian back in 1960/61.

Clive Bennett *[the author]*

In addition to these long serving folk enthusiasts I have also been deeply involved with the folk scene since 1961. My involvement, over some 40 years, has however been quite varied. After co-organising the first Brighton Folk Club in 1961 I was, as described elsewhere in this book, involved at various times with organising song clubs in Worthing [1962 and 1967-73], Shoreham [1963-64], Brighton [1962-63 and 1979-81], Eastbourne [1973-81], Lewes [1979] and Seaford [1978 and 1992 to date] along with 24 years as Bagman to The Merrie England Mummers. During the mid 1960's I lived in Kent where I organised Folkestone's first folk club [1964-67], Canterbury's first and hugely successful Pilgrim's Way Folk Song Club [1964-67], the first Ashford Folk Club [1966] and Deal Folk Club [1967].

The Author at Worthing Folk Club 1972
the author

My enthusiasm for folk music grew from an interest in traditional jazz and the skiffle craze of the late 1950's and my early influences were Burl Ives and the legendary American blues singer Big Bill Broonzy whom I saw perform at The Dome, Brighton during his last European tour in 1957. These eventually led to my involvement with club organising after meeting Terry Scarlett and our partnership in running, briefly, a song club in East Preston and the founding of The Southern Folk Music Society.

Since 1962 I have been a member of the English Folk Dance and Song Society [EFDSS] and have also been involved with various folk activities at national level. In 1965, at a folk club organiser's conference in Manchester, I was a founder member and elected to the National Executive of the British Federation of Folk Clubs [BFFC], an autonomous national association of folk song clubs, operating under the auspices of the EFDSS. The following year I was elected Vice Chairman – a position I held for four years until succeeding to the Chair from 1971 to 1975. During this time the BFFC was responsible for the development of the National Festival, initially at Keele and then Loughborough Universities. From 1973 to 1979 I served on the National Executive of the EFDSS and its Artistic Development Committee and in 1975 was one of the four-man committee responsible for the creation of the Folk Promenade concerts at the Royal Albert Hall, London. In addition I also served on both the Sussex [1963/4 and 1969/73] and Kent [1965/6] District Committees of the Society. In 1966 I was invited to become the first Song Producer of Broadstairs Folk Show, a post I held for four years. A decade later, in 1976, when the EFDSS took over sponsorship of the event and renamed it Broadstairs Folk Festival I was again involved in a similar capacity for two years.

Like virtually all those already mentioned I am neither a native of Brighton nor indeed Sussex. I was born in north-east Hertfordshire during 1934 into a small rural community in the village of Barley set in a fold in the East Anglian Heights astride the junction of two ancient routes, one running from Ware to Cambridge and the other from the local market town of Royston to Saffron Walden. The village, which is mentioned in The Domesday Book, had only some 250 inhabitants, but there were five pubs, a village blacksmith and a wheelwright.

My maternal grandfather was a saddle and harness maker, living in Ware while my paternal roots were deep in the local soil where the family had worked as farm labourers or shepherds in Barley or the hamlet of Wyddial for over 250 years. My father however was a gardener, although during the Second World War, as this was not an essential occupation, he worked for six years as a farm labourer. I remember taking lunch to him in the harvest fields during the summer and in the autumn leading a team of horses back and forth across the field whilst he trudged behind guiding a heavy plough. I also recall how, after school, I would go along to the smithy and pump the bellows for the blacksmiths while they were shoeing horses or repairing a set of harrows.

I grew up at a time before the television screen invaded every household, when the emphasis was on entertaining yourself and, like many others, music was an important part of our family life. Sunday evenings and Christmas were times for family gatherings around the piano with songs and music, for mine was very much a musical family. My mother played the piano, my father the violin and also sang in the choir of the local chapel where my grandmother was the organist. After attending Letchworth Grammar School I went to Cambridge Art School before moving to Sussex in 1952. Three years later, following National Service in the Royal Air Force, I joined the newly nationalised South Eastern Electricity Board where I worked for the next 39 years, much of the time as a Procurement and Contracts Officer.

During 1977 I was admitted to the Chartered Institute of Purchasing and Supply and in 1992 gained a Bachelor of Arts Degree in Social Science from the Open University. An active trade unionist I spent many years as a NALGO, and its successor UNISON, branch officer and was South East Electricity Branch Chairperson from 1985 until my retirement in 1993 since when I have been Branch President.

Today, in the first year of the new millennium, whilst Vic and Tina Smith, Sandra Goddard and myself, after forty years, remain active in running folk clubs in the area and Terry Masterson and Miles Wootton are still to be heard singing in the local clubs, things have changed. The new city of Brighton and Hove is totally bereft of a formal folk club, apart from a Saturday evening singaround session, although within the general area covered by this book there are still well established clubs running in Lewes, Seaford and Eastbourne with new clubs at Southwick and Worthing. Elsewhere there are still regular folk sessions in Horsham, Chichester, Arundel, Steyning and Turners Hill [near Crawley].

8   KEY INDIVIDUALS

THE TRADITIONAL PERFORMERS

It seems appropriate to end where we began with the long history of singing and music in Sussex. The oft quoted comment by Cecil Sharp in his book 'English Folk Song, Some Conclusions' published in 1907 that the old [traditional] singers were a dying breed and that *"In less than a decade, therefore, English folk singing will be extinct"* has long been disproved and nowhere more clearly than in Sussex.

In the late 50's Bob Copper, working for the BBC, collected material from a number of singers in Sussex, including Harold 'Jim' Swain from Angmering who worked as a carter-boy when young but lost his sight at an early age through an influenza epidemic, George Attrill of Fittleworth a former farm worker then employed by West Sussex County Council as a roadman, Noah Gillette from Hastings and inshore fisherman Ned 'Wintry' Adams of Hollington. More details of his collecting are to be found in his excellent book "Songs and Southern Breezes" published in 1973.

A few years after Bob's collecting trips the folk revival of the 1960's was still early enough for those in and around Brighton who were interested in traditional music to hear at first hand some outstanding local source singers such as 'Pop' Maynard, Harry Holman, Jim Wilson, George Townshend, Scan Tester, George Spicer, George Belton and Johnny Doughty thereby maintaining continuity with the past.

From the mid 1950's onward many lesser known performers were collected, particularly by Mervyn Plunkett, Reg Hall, Mike Yates and Ken Stubbs and made public during the mid 70's through the release of several Topic records "Sussex Harvest", "When Sheepshearing's Done", "Green Grow the Laurels", "Songs of The Open Road" and "Songs and Southern Breezes". More details of these early recording sessions can be found in the booklet accompanying the Musical Traditions double disc MTCD 309-10 "Just Another Saturday Night" released in 2001 and in Reg Hall's excellent book on Scan Tester, mentioned later.

In addition to the better known singers already mentioned these recordings include Ernest 'Rabbidy' Baxter, Harry Upton and Mary Ann Haynes. 'Rabbidy' Baxter from Chelwood Gate, who accompanied Scan Tester on tambourine, was working as a gardener when Bill Leader recorded him at the Half Moon, Balcombe in 1962. Harry Upton, a part time cowman living in Balcombe, was recorded by Mike Yates in the early 70's. He was born in 1900 and learnt many of his songs as a boy both from his mother and father, a Downsland shepherd, along with his father's work-mates and friends, including the Coppers of Rottingdean. Mary Ann Haynes, a former gypsy then living in a tower block flat in the centre of Brighton, was born on 9 April 1903 in a gypsy waggon behind a pub in Portsmouth. She spent much of her early life travelling the country visiting fairs with her horse-dealer father. Following the early death of her husband she reared a large family single-handed and for many years ran a flower stall in Brighton.

The Cherry Tree at Copthorne hosted a number of traditional song sessions that were organised, as Jim Ward, a revival singer from the Crawley area, described them, "for the benefit of the folk academics who usually outnumbered the singers ferried in from outlying areas for the event". Performers, such as 'Pop' Maynard, George Spicer and Harry Holman, were then expected to sing 'proper' folk songs and to exclude the other items that made up their full repertoire. Ken Stubbs and Mike Yates attended these sessions and as Jim Ward, again, recalls, Ken Stubbs, in later years reflected on how silly he had been to not have recorded the Victorian and Music Hall songs these singers knew.

As mentioned earlier, Brian Matthews, on his field trips, recorded a number of singers and of these, two not mentioned in detail later in this chapter, are Harry Holman and Jim 'Brick' Harber. Harry, a great friend of 'Pop' Maynard, was a part time gardener and potman at the Cherry Tree in Copthorne where he lived. His family had been involved with farming for generations although he had formerly worked on the railway. 'Brick' Harber, who although born in Worcestershire, had moved to Tilgate Forest with his gamekeeper father when about six years of age. He had spent most of his life in the Forest as a charcoal-burner and working at other trades related to timber.

For the regular club audiences however, even as late as the 1990's almost a century after Sharp's comments, there were still traditional performers such as The Coppers, Ron Spicer and Gordon Hall singing, not only in their own environment, but out and about as guests in the local folk clubs.

Vic Smith noted in the Mid Sussex Times on 3 June 1976 that *"The folk clubs of the Sussex area seem to be very conscious of the debt that they owe to the various old country singers who have been the source of so much of their material, and the relationship between some of the country singers and the folk clubs appears to be very good. At least, they go along to sing at the clubs. For example, tonight at the Coppersong Folk Club at the Central Club in South Coast Road, Peacehaven, the guests are George Spicer and Cyril Phillips, and tomorrow night at the Springfield Hotel folk club, Brighton you can hear George Belton and Bob Lewis."*

To end this book I would like to recall details of some of the great singers who could be heard in Sussex during the forty years since the folk revival arrived in Brighton. This is a mixture of personal memories from various singers and information culled from record sleeve notes although, as Jim Ward says, these should not always be relied upon as correct.

Reflecting on record sleeve notes Jim Ward said "I kept in touch with George [Spicer] as I used his local, the Punch Bowl at Turners Hill, in the mid-sixties". "George's notes ["When Sheepshearing's Done] give the impression that he and Harry Holman were great mates. George met Harry at the Cherry Tree and many years later [around 1970/71] I gave George a lift to Ken's [Stubbs] session at Marsh Green. This was the first time George had been to any kind of 'folk' sing song for about seven years and Harry Holman was there and so was Mike Yates. This may be where the sleeve notes originated."

George 'Pop' Maynard, Copthorne 1872-1962

'Pop' Maynard as everyone called him was born in Smallfield in 1872 but spent most of his life in the nearby village of Copthorne where he died in 1962 at the age of ninety. He acquired the nickname 'Pop' not because of his age [his father Jim was still alive in 1948 and George was known as 'Pop' even then] but through his skill as a marble player and the ability to 'pop' the marbles out of the ring.

George Maynard 'popping' marbles
Brian Matthews

Singing was an integral part of his everyday existence and many of his songs were learnt within the family circle.

Although his formal education was, typically for that time, short he did learn to read. As a result, in addition to the many songs he learnt from his father, brothers and sisters, his repertoire was expanded beyond this oral transmission by hand written texts and ballad sheets which were hawked round the villages. He was also blessed with a prodigious memory and acquired a vast repertoire of traditional and music hall songs.

Before the second World War Copthorne residents, known locally as 'Yellowbellies', were generally seen as a lawless bunch and expert poachers and George was no exception. Although he had a reputation as a hard working, reliable and skilful labourer, able to carry out the full range of farm works; harvesting by hand, hedging, ditching, hop picking and woodcutting and through this always being able to earn an honest living, in times of hardship it might well have been supplemented with poaching game.

He worked more or less full-time until he was nearly eighty years old and his last full-time job was as a woodcutter on the Rowfant estate.

He had been happily married although for almost half his life he was a widower and after his four sons and two daughters left home he lived on his own until the final years when he lived with his daughter. Only in the final year or two of his life, after many of his friends had died, was he heard to acknowledge being a little lonely.

With his white beard and bicycle he was a familiar figure around the village where he was viewed with the reverence of a patriarch.

Brian Matthews and Dick Richardson, both of whom performed at the original Brighton Ballads and Blues Club in the autumn of 1961 visited 'Pop' regularly and learnt songs from him while Jim Ward lived in the area and visited the sessions at the Cherry Tree

Song collector Ken Stubbs rated George as the greatest traditional singer discovered after the Second World War. George was recorded by the BBC at The Cherry Tree, Copthorne which was then transmitted as part of their 'As I Roved Out' series. Before being discovered by the folk world however he was already a celebrity not only from his singing but also, to a much wider audience, through his sporting exploits at shove-ha'penny, quoits, darts and particularly marbles. In 1948 his team won the traditional annual marbles championship held at Tinsley Green near Crawley on Good Friday and in subsequent years he was seen on TV shooting his marbles.

Topic Records issued 12T286 '*Ye Subjects of England*' in 1976 a consisting wholly of songs by George and he can also be heard on Collector JEB7 '*Four Sussex Singers*' released in 1961

Jim Wilson, Three Bridges 1875-1961
Jim, who lived with his son at Three Bridges, had once worked as a miller's roundsman and later, until he retired, on the railway after which he took gardening jobs. He was a regular at the Plough at Three Bridges where they often had a sing-song and although less well known outside his own area he was recorded by Mervyn Plunkett in 1961 who wrote: *"Jim Wilson is over eighty and is a gardener by trade. He has a fair repertoire of country songs and knows perhaps another hundred fragments. His singing is highly stylised and his stentorian voice can bring order to the noisiest bar-parlour."*

George Townshend, Lewes 1882-1967
George Townshend was born at Wootten Farm, East Chiltington near Lewes on 29 August 1882, the only boy in a family of seven children. His father was a farm bailiff but he left the land when George was seven years old and took over the village pub, 'The Jolly Sportsman' where, every Saturday evening there was singing in the bar. It was here that George first performed in public when, on

the day his father opened the pub the pair of them stood side by side and sang "Those Glittering Dewdrops" and "When Spring Comes In".

As a boy George was in the church choir and on Sunday evenings he and his sisters would sing to their father, who seldom attended the service, the hymns they had sung in church earlier in the day.

At the age of eleven George took up playing the melodeon, the only member of his family who played an instrument, but by the time of the folk revival he was no longer playing it.

After four years at the pub his father returned to the land, concentrating on fattening cattle and several times a week George would help his father to take them off to the local market.

George Townshend at Horsham Festival 1961 *Tony Wales*

George started work as a carter boy, walking alongside the lead horse in all kinds of weather but at the age of sixteen he had two horses of his own and went ploughing with a single furrow plough.

In 1901 after a disagreement with his father he left and went to work for the Brighton and South Coast railway as a timekeeper at the Engineer's Office, earning a wage of eighteen shillings [90 pence] a week with privilege tickets and three days holiday a year.

He married a local girl in 1908 and also joined the Volunteer Company of the Royal Garrison Artillery where he rose to the rank of sergeant. In 1914 he joined up as a full time soldier and was sent to France to fight in the First World War. When the war ended he returned to the railway and joined the railway police.

Later, when he retired, George worked as a court usher in Lewes and for recreation did odd job gardening, went walking on the Downs or watched steeplechase racing and fox hunting. His wife died around 1952 and after that he then went to live in Lewes with one of his two daughters. He also had one son.

George learnt a lot of his songs from his father who in turn had learnt them from his mother. Both Tony Wales and song collector Ken Stubbs recorded George and collected a number of interesting songs from him. Even into his eighties George retained a strong, clear voice which delighted listeners and I remember George, at the age of seventy-nine, singing his favourite song "Those

Glittering Dewdrop" at Horsham Festival in 1961, an item captured on the ARCO/Folk Bag Limited Edition 12" long playing record Number F.B.12.101 titled 'Welcome to the Festival', which also has a photograph of George on the sleeve.

George died in Southampton on 18 February 1967 at the age of eighty-four. A Musical Traditions CD, MTCD 304 *'Come Hand to Me the Glass'* based on recordings of George made by Brian Matthews was issued in 2000.

Lewis 'Scan' Tester, Horsted Keynes 1887-1972

'Scan' Tester was an acknowledged master of the Anglo-Concertina and a wonderful raconteur. His instrumental skill extended to playing the melodeon, tin whistle, the rare Bandolian – a large concertina and he was also an accomplished fiddler. Born on 7 September 1887 at Chelwood Common, Sussex, the second youngest of eight children, he grew up in a public house when his father took The Green Man at Horsted Keynes in 1891. Saturday evening bar entertainment included music, singing and step dancing and it was there that he learnt many of the tunes that were to form part of his superb repertoire.

By the age of eight he could play the tambourine well enough to accompany his uncle and brother when they went out playing music at various pubs and it was through this that he acquired a nickname. Scan was of relatively small stature and on one occasion, as they were getting off a cart, someone mused that Lewis was grown up enough to play music but too small to get down from the tail of a cart unaided. Giving him a hand down he said "Come here, you little scantiloper!" and 'Scan' was to stay with him for life.

Scan Tester at Keele Folk Festival 1965
Brian Shuel ["Collections"]

While the pub provided a steady income, supplemented by selling ponies bred in the paddock at the rear, the main family business was twofold. One as licensed fish hawkers, selling their harvest from the sea around local farms and cottages; the other was brickmaking, with three brickfields at Horsted Keynes and Newick. As a young man, at a time when life was far from easy, Scan

174

recalls walking six miles to work in the brick-fields to earn a wage of fourpence an hour. But the walking didn't last too long he added, he asked for and got an extra half-penny an hour and hired a bicycle.

Scan's uncle Tom and elder brother Tranter both played concertina and so it was perhaps almost inevitable that young Scan should also adopt the instrument. In the late summer he and his brother used to go hop picking at Iden Green in Kent and here they would spend the evenings plying their instruments to entertain the 'hoppers'. Scan recalls that they earned their keep by playing and only drew their picking money at the end of the season. Step dancing was a popular pastime and both the Tester brothers became expert at both the stepping and the playing.

His first job outside the family business was as an assistant groundsman, preparing cricket pitches at Brook House in Ashdown Forest where he also played cricket on a regular basis until after the First World War. He supplemented his income with wood cutting and trimming bracken and heather in the forest. He would also go off, sleeping rough and busking around pubs. There were also visits to Brighton to busk on the sea front and Johnny Doughty, a local fisherman, recalls seeing him playing music amidst the fishermen.

When he was 22 years old Scan married and in 1910 they had a daughter, Daisy. Scan then worked for a building firm in Crowborough, walking a round trip of 10 miles or more each day. Meanwhile the family business had come to an end following his father's death in 1916. His wife died in 1917 and Scan became a sawyer, working for a timber merchant and living in a caravan at Horam Road railway station. He re-married in 1920 and then moved to Horam.

While the death of his first wife brought one musical career to an end his re-marrying opened up a new musical experience. During the late nineteen twenties and early thirties Scan's music became a popular part of Sussex life with the formation of his own band comprising himself on concertina and fiddle, his wife on the drums, their daughter on the piano and his two brothers also on concertinas with the eldest doubling up on clarinet. They played for dances at local villages, performing polkas, waltzes, quadrilles, the veleta and the lancers. The same line up also played jazz under the name of Tester's Imperial Jazzband. After the depression of the thirties they played mainly at home and this phase of his musical life ended in 1953 when his second wife died.

Scan spent virtually all his working and musical life around Horsted Keynes but in 1957 was 'discovered' by Mervyn Plunkett and Reg Hall, fiddle player with The Rakes country dance band and in his latter days Scan made trips, in the company of Reg, to the Fox at Islington and the Bedford at Camden Town. He was an occasional visitor to the Horsham Songswappers Club, appeared at the early Horsham Folk Festivals and also guested at the Keele Folk Festival – forerunner of The National Festival, now an annual event at Loughborough University.

Watching him it was amazing that his gnarled fingers could play anything but they danced over the buttons of his instrument producing superb tunes, made all the more remarkable by the fact that he could read not one note of music. As the folk revival developed during the early 1960's and Scan's fame grew, numerous musicians came to visit and listen to a master musician. Scan died, aged eighty-five, on 7 May 1972 at Horsted Keynes. His concertina is now owned by Will Duke, mentioned earlier.

For more detailed accounts of Scan's life see two published items. An article by Chris Duff in the 'Brighton Folk Diary' Number 13, January/February 1971 and 'Musical Traditions' Supplement No. 2 "*I Never Played to Many Posh Dances*" by Reg Hall published in 1990. The latter also covers collecting from various other musicians and singers found in the High Weald area of central Sussex during the late nineteen-fifties and early nineteen-sixties together with social context and comment.

George Belton, Madehurst 1898-1980

George was born at Oxted in Surrey in 1898 the youngest of five children and spent most of his early life around Redhill as his father who was a carter moved from farm to farm.

Throughout his life George worked with horses. He was a champion ploughman winning over eighty prizes in various competitions. As late as 1967, well past normal retirement age, George was helping manage and run a small farm at Madehurst, near Arundel in West Sussex and it was from here that he made regular visits to the Horsham Songswappers club.

George Belton at Madehurst, Easter 1965
the author

Mrs Mary Baron who owned the farm was a devotee of traditional music and made regular visits to Horsham for the folk evenings, usually with one or two of her companions from the all female household. It was she who took 'Belton', as she always called him, along to the club in 1960. As George recalled he arrived, somewhat apprehensively, at the hall and climbed the stairs "Wondering what this folk singing was all about." He waited outside for Harry Mousdell to finish singing 'I Wish I Were Single Again' before entering.

176

In that moment he thought, "Oh, if it's that type of song then I'm all right" and thereafter he was a regular and popular visitor.

He had an incredible memory and a vast stock of songs, many learnt from his parents and family, but was always ready to add a new one to his repertoire. Having heard Sydney Carter sing "Mixed Up Old Man" George quickly learnt it and sang it with glee. Like virtually all country singers he knew a number of music hall songs, although rather fewer than most. He regularly amazed his listeners by producing a previously unheard song or version of a song, often in response to hearing something sung by another singer. His enthusiasm was infectious, his pleasure in singing was obvious and he was frequently asked to 'warm up' the audience at the start of a folk gathering. Large audiences never worried him, whatever the venue informal or formal he was always completely relaxed and at ease with his songs. At festivals be it under canvas at Reading or open air at Lewes or even a lecture room at the National in Loughborough – where he was a regular and honoured performer – his unselfconscious personality was an object lesson for any aspiring singer. This was well demonstrated when he attended a packed concert by the Spinners at Portsmouth Guildhall and they invited him up on stage for a song. He didn't hesitate and showed not the slightest sign of nerves as he sang.

George's frequent visits to clubs and festivals made him well known to many singers around the Brighton folk scene, in particular Paul Setford, Bob Lewis, Harry Mousdell and myself all of whom learnt from him "The Sussex Toast" a song which he learnt as a young man whilst working on a farm on the Surrey, Sussex border.

> *I have drunk one and I will drink two*
> *There stands one who drank as much as you*
> *For he's been and done as the rest have done*
> *Him and his good companions*
> And so on, rhyming numbers up to ten

Several of his other songs were great favourites with local audiences and he was often asked for The Dark Eyed Sailor, Jim the Carter Lad and Barbara Allen. Vic Smith remembers George's singing of The Bold Fisherman with affection since it concentrated his thoughts on the local traditional performers when he had previously used mainly Scottish and Irish source singers as guests at the Lewes Pug O' Junch club.

When George eventually retired he moved to Selsey and in 1974 at the age of seventy-eight started writing regular articles about the country life of his youth for the Sussex folk magazine 'Plum Heavy'. He died on 11 January 1980 at the age of eighty-one.

George was recorded by the English Folk Dance and Song Society for its archives and a number of tracks were released on their record E.F.D.S.S. Folk Classic LP1008 *"All Jolly Fellows"* issued 1967. He can also be heard on tracks of Transatlantic XTRA: XTRS 1150 *"The Brave Ploughboy"* issued in 1974

George Edward Spicer, 1906-1981

George Spicer was born at Little Chart, Kent in 1906 and left school at the age of fourteen when he went to work on a local farm as a general farmhand. After two years he became an under herdsman and at the age of twenty-six the head man. His early working life was spent on farms in the Dover and Deal area and continued on various farms in Kent near Faversham, Canterbury, Maidstone and Biggin Hill before moving to Selsfield, Sussex in 1940 where he was employed as head herdsman with pedigree Guernsey cattle. Here he was to work for virtually all of the next thirty-one years until

retiring in 1971. George had a vast store of songs ranging from music hall tear jerkers to comic songs and classic traditional ballads. Many he learnt from his parents, others from various relatives and still more from pub singsongs. After retiring he remained very active as a part time gamekeeper, village cricket umpire and enthusiastic gardener, he won over one thousand certificates at various flower shows for his skills.

George Spicer *Mrs Doris Spicer*

A renowned singer, with a fine commanding voice, throughout his life, George performed in village pubs at sing arounds including various hostelries around the Ashdown Forest area. During the 1950's he regularly took his son Ron along to play accordion while he did the singing. However Brian Matthews remembers him not only as "a powerful singer who would dominate most pub sing-songs" but also that this was often "much to the annoyance of other singers"

The collector Ken Stubbs maintained that George was never 'discovered' by song collectors. He insisted George was so well known as a singer that anyone visiting the area in search of traditional material could not help but find him. Vic Smith, in the Mid Sussex Times of 30 September 1976 said *"There is a real magic In the way he* [George] *delivers a song like 'The Barley Mow'. This song which often sounds hackneyed and dull from the mouths of most singers, takes on a new exhilarating life in the way that George sings it."* The next year, on 3 February, in the same paper Vic reported that George *"... has a poor opinion of his own voice which others rate so highly."* Going on to say that George gave the Victorian parlour ballads 'The Old Rustic Bridge' and Volunteer Organist' as his own favourites.

George died at Selsfield, Sussex in 1981 at the age of seventy-five. He made one complete record for Topic, 12T235 "Blackberry Fold" released in 1974 and may also be heard on tracks of several others, Collector JEB7 *"Four Sussex Singers"* issued in 1961 and Topic 12T254 *"When Sheepshearing's Done"* released in 1975

Johnny Doughty, Rye 1903-1985

Within the context of this book Johnny Doughty is of particular interest since he was born in a cottage now demolished, in Wellington Place, Brighton, in the centre of what was then the town's fishing district, on 1 September 1903

Brought up largely by his grandmother, who took in washing, he recalled how she used to spend all day at her tub washing and singing, in the process teaching the young Johnny many of his first songs. All of his spare time he spent on the beach with the old sailors. At first with the cockles and whelks stalls then helping empty boats of their catches. Here he listened to tales of the sea and sea lore, how to steer a boat and rhymes about navigation.

Johnny Doughty
Mike Yates

Johnny left school at thirteen and went herring catching for the next two years before joining the Royal Navy in May 1919. He was invalided out after an accident but it was difficult to earn a living from fishing because of the depression so he went to work in the gashouse at Portslade for £4 a week. From this he saved enough money to buy a second hand boat and when he left the gas works they gave him £45 pension money with which he had two new boats built. From then until the start of the second world war he used them to take holiday fishermen and trippers round the bay in summer and for his own fishing in winter.

At the start of the war he volunteered for the Royal Navy and eventually became bos'n on a fuel tanker. When this was bombed he escaped uninjured and joined a minesweeper which became victim of a mine. In 1945, whilst on leave, he was asked to take a converted trawler from Shoreham to Rye harbour and with the end of the war he settled in Rye working on his own boats until retiring.

Such a background inevitably gave him a vast repertoire of songs learnt as a boy from the old fishermen singing whilst mending nets on Brighton Beach. Others he learnt from his family and neighbours and colleagues at sea. They range from ballads to locally composed songs. To this add personal charm and wit and a great sense of fun coupled with the ability to hold an audience with wonderful stories, some true some tall.

'Discovered' in his mid 70's he was a revelation at the ill fated Brighton 1977 Folk Festival and subsequently became well known to many revival singers in the Brighton area, making a number of guest appearances at local clubs. Johnny had an exuberant personality, he was a great story teller and a singer of clarity and vigour which had made him something of a legend among the Sussex fishing community even before his emergence into the folk world in the 1970's. After this he became a firm favourite at national festivals and folk clubs around the country to which he was frequently driven by Eddie Upton. He died in Rye on 21 September 1985 at the age of eighty-two.

Johnny is featured on Topic Records 12TS324 *"Round Rye Bay for More"* issued in 1977.

Cyril Philips, Firle 1911-1990

Cyril Phillips was born in Dorset on 5 November 1911 but whilst still a small boy his father moved not just the family but the entire farm, by train, to Firle in Sussex. There, Cyril left school at the age of fourteen to work on his father's farm.

Cyril Phillips at a pub session, July 1987 *Tony Wales*

He learnt his songs in the villages and farms of Sussex and between the wars was a regular performer in village smoking concerts, harvest suppers and local pubs. Although in later life he suffered from increasing deafness, which could result in playing one key whilst singing in another, and was also handicapped in his playing by arthritis in his hands even his most severe critic nevertheless had to admit that he gave much pleasure to his audience with the unbridled zeal which typified his performance.

He delighted in the folk revival, adapting easily to mix with the new young enthusiast for the old songs and visited many clubs and festivals often as chauffeur to other singers and Scan Tester, George Spicer and George Belton all told hair-raising stories of his particular style of driving.

After his wife's death he retired from his farm at Firle and roamed the world sending home hilarious letters of his latest escapades. He was a great raconteur and at home was always much in demand at village gatherings not just for his songs but also for his traditional stories and reminiscences which he had gathered at home and abroad during his life.

He was a gregarious, warm hearted and generous person with an individualistic, larger than life personality who was always welcome wherever he went.

Cyril can be heard on Transatlantic Records XTRS1150 *'The Brave Ploughboy'* issued in 1975

Ron Spicer, Ardingly 1929 -1996

Son of George Spicer, Ron was born at West Langdon near Dover, Kent on 12 January 1929 and died in Crawley, Sussex on 26 November 1996 at the age of sixty-six.

Ron Spicer at Lewes Folk Club 1996
Jim Marshall

A reserved and quiet man Ron, although an accomplished accordion player and singer, was content to stay in the background while his illustrious father was alive. After his death Ron, at the age of fifty-three and after a visit to the folk club at Three Bridges, took up the mantle of maintaining the old songs – but in his own way, not as the son of George. He quickly absorbed the skill of standing up in public, be it festival, concert or folk club and charming an audience with his interpretation of a song. In keeping with all the old singers he was never slow to learn a new song traditional or contemporary if he thought it worth singing. He developed rapidly into a confident and popular performer and was admired by folk enthusiasts far beyond the borders of his adopted Sussex for his subtle and persuasive style.

Ron began playing the melodeon at the age of five and the first one he owned was bought by his grandmother. He progressed to the accordion and at the age of fourteen bought himself a 42-bass instrument with which he went to Turners Hill every Saturday night to entertain the Canadian soldiers in the local pubs. In 1943 he left school and went to work as gardener alongside his grandfather who was also a melodeon player and a source from which he learnt many tunes. He progressed to herdsman and when his father retired succeeded him as head herdsman, remaining on the same farm for all his life. He attended various country shows and became a respected cattle judge at the annual South of England Agricultural Show held at Ardingly.

His untimely death from cancer at the comparatively early age of sixty-six whilst at the height of his popularity was a sad loss to the folk world nation-wide but particularly Sussex where he, accompanied by Doris his wife of forty-two years, was a visitor to one or other of the local clubs virtually every night of the week.

For further information see his biography *"The Life Of A Man"* published by Country Books 1997. Ron can be heard on Veteran Tapes CD *"When The May is All in Bloom"*, the Steel Carpet tape *"Keys of Canterbury"* and *"Following My Dear Old Dad"* a tape released when Country Books published his biography.

Bob Blake, Broadbridge Heath 1908-1991

Bob Blake was a man of many diverse interests and abilities. He was born at Tooting on 29 December 1908 when it was on the outer fringe of London but spent virtually all his life in the country. He was introduced to folk music at an early age when his father, who had been a windjammer sailor with many years' experience in the China Sea, taught him Sea Shanties. Then, during school holidays, he took him to visit his uncle in Gloucestershire, another ex sailor, who played concertina and also sang many old songs.

Bob served an apprenticeship as a coach trimmer and at the age of nineteen moved to Brook's Green, near Horsham. There he started work as a trimmer in a local garage and lodged with an elderly couple at a nearby farm. As their health deteriorated he also helped out around the farm. He moved to Tower Hill in 1938 when he married a local girl and from her grandmother learnt much about the country life of Sussex.

Bob was always fond of the outdoor life and enjoyed cycling, camping, canoeing and was also a keen photographer – his camera accompanied him everywhere. As his daughter Sylvia Parsons recalls he would suddenly strap his camping gear on the bike and disappear for a few days. Distance was no deterrent and he often cycled from Horsham down to the New Forest noting in his diaries details of the views, birds and people he saw along the way.

He also joined the Auxiliary Fire Service in Horsham as a part time fireman, then when the war started, instead of being allowed to follow his father into the Navy he was conscripted to what was to become the National Fire Service. Fortunately he was stationed in Horsham with the job of locating water sources and consequently knew every river, stream and pond in the county.

Bob Blake [c1971]
Mrs S Parsons [née Blake]

During the 1940's he learnt the new language Esperanto and acquired a host of pen friends all over the world. This led to several trips abroad taking his beloved bike with him on the ferry. Then by train to Holland, Germany or Spain where he would explore the local countryside.

He would also bundle the whole family into the Austin 7, and take off for camping holidays in Norfolk or the New Forest or weekend jaunts along the river Arun at Pulborough where he kept a small boat. His most ambitious venture was to undertake a cycle tour of Ireland with his fifteen-year-old son.

Throughout his life he was a great naturalist and spent many hours observing and photographing wildlife, particularly badgers. He kept bees at many locations around Sussex and in the 1950's took over an apiary in Southwater woods. There he could often be found at night with a huge lantern collecting moths and other insects attracted by the light. Bob also kept bees in the New Forest where he befriended a Forest Vendurer and was given permission to camp anywhere in the Forest, something not usually allowed.

In 1957 the family moved to Dragon's Green in Shipley where Bob was employed as a gardener, but he was soon helping out on the farm or anywhere else where he was needed.

When he retired he and his wife moved to Broadbridge Heath and although his health was by then not good he still went off on cycling holidays well into his seventies. He also took up repairing antique furniture. On receiving a pair of bellows in need of repair, and after a great deal of research, he learnt to make replica antique bellows and became proficient at embossing leather. He was an accomplished artist and most of his designs were of animals. He also tried pottery and then progressed to modelling finely detailed woodland creatures out of clay.

After moving to Sussex in the 1920's Bob extended his repertoire of traditional songs and in the period between the two World Wars would cycle miles around Sussex if he heard about someone who knew some old songs, or even a particular verse he was looking for. However he tended to specialise in the songs of the great Horsham singer Henry Burstow. Bob's family didn't realise just how much of a collector he was until after his death when, as his daughter Sylvia remembers, they discovered a large quantity of manuscripts recording his collecting work.

Bob was also a musician and played the violin but it was as a singer that he became an immensely popular and regular performer at the Horsham Songswappers club, also appearing at the Horsham Festivals of the early 1960's. Several times he appeared with Bob Copper and his family and in 1975 he was included on two folk compilation albums released by Topic Records, *"Sussex Harvest"* and *"When Sheepshearing's Done"*. He died from cancer, on 20 January 1991 aged eighty-two.

Clare Clayton [née KilBride], Ditchling Common 1929-

Clare was born at Ditchling Common, Sussex in 1929 the second eldest of five children. She grew up in the village where her father was a craftsman silk weaver with premises within the Guild of St Joseph and Dominic, a group of Catholic craftsmen operating from a collection of small workshops. Her parents were members of the local Chapel and at Christmas the men went carol singing round the neighbourhood with a small wooden crib. There was also the Feast of St Dominic in August with a day of festivities and sport culminating in a supper at the Royal Oak, Ditchling Common at which there was always singing and it was at these events that as a child Clare first started to learn folk songs.

Clare Clayton and Jenny KilBride
Terry Masterson

Clare's mother was a Scot from Banffshire while her father, although born in Bradford, was of Irish descent, his father being a surgeon from Cork.

During the 1939-45 war the family moved to her mother's native Scotland where her father worked on a farm for much of the time as he was unable to obtain silk for weaving. He did however maintain some weaving, creating woollen habits for monasteries. Clare meanwhile attended school in Aberdeen. Whilst north of the border she again encountered folk singing and extended her repertoire of traditional material. After the war the family moved back to Sussex and having left school she worked as a weaver on her father's hand loom at Ditchling where, from the next workshop, she could hear the singing of the stonemason Joseph Cribb, a fine performer, again of traditional material.

After her marriage in 1955 she stopped work to concentrate on raising a family and moved to Hassocks where she has lived ever since. Two other singers in particular she recalls left lasting impressions. First, a gypsy family who called one Christmas, singing carols on the doorstep in a harsh, somehow mid European style and secondly, whilst attending a folk weekend organised by the English Folk dance and Song Society at Lodge Hill near Pulborough where the guest was the legendary American singer Jean Ritchie.

In 1961 she was invited to perform as a solo singer at the Horsham folk festival but decided to include her two brothers, Thomas and Gilbert – her elder brother having unfortunately been killed in a flying accident in 1952 whilst serving National Service. Having been raised on plainsong they quickly developed a repertoire and were soon recognised as accomplished harmony singers.

During the autumn of 1962 Clare, from time to time accompanied by either or both of her brothers, was one of the residents at the original Brighton Ballads and Blues club meeting in Fuller's Restaurant in East Street. Then in 1967, after her brothers had moved away, she teamed up with Derek Lockwood both to sing and run the monthly folk club at the New Inn, Hurstpierpoint. She was also joined from time to time by her young sister Jenny KilBride.

Margaret Louise 'Louie' Fuller [née Brooks], Lingfield 1916 -

Louie was born in Woolwich, London, on 6 June 1916 where her father worked at Woolwich Arsenal and she recalls her mother's concern about the occasional bombing raid on the area towards the end of the First World War. Most of her early life however was spent in the Ladbroke Grove area of West London.

Like many Londoners her family took her hop picking in Kent during the late summer and there she spent her leisure hours singing and story telling at hop picker gatherings and family parties where she learnt many songs, particularly from her parents. From an early age she was always singing and remembers, at the age of fourteen, someone coming to the house to collect her – along with the boy next door – to go and sing a duet on stage at the London Palladium. She is not sure what the show was but it was, she says, just the one performance. From her description however it would seem likely that it was one of the Scout Association's 'Gang Shows'.

Louie Fuller, Feb 2001 *the author*

It was in the hop fields during the late summer of 1932, at the age of sixteen, that she met William 'Bill' Saunders a member of an Irish travelling family who was, as Louie recalls, a popular and very good step dancer. At the end of the season she told her parents she was not going back to London. Instead she left with Bill, some sixteen years her senior, with all their belongings strapped to his bike while she sat on the crossbar.

For a while they lived in a tent but soon bought a horse and van [gypsy caravan]. She adopted the life of a traveller and together with Bill worked at a variety of jobs round the farms of Kent and Sussex before eventually settling in a static caravan provided by the farmer they were then working for. At the beginning of the second World War they moved from Four Elms, Kent into a rather primitive bungalow, with no running water, deep in Bakers Wood, Newchapel on the Surrey and Sussex border where Bill worked as a woodcutter.

Although the first of their four children was born within the first year of their life together it was not until 1944 that they finally got married.

In 1960, just one week before his sixtieth birthday Bill died. Within five years however Louie moved to Lingfield to live with and then marry Henry Fuller, one of Bill's friends. Unlike Bill, Henry was not a traveller but was born and lived all his life in the town. Henry enjoyed Louie's singing and would always go with her to any singsong where he sang along with her. He died in 1986 at the age of eighty-four but the diminutive Louie continues to live in their bungalow in Lingfield.

She still sings at folk clubs, including the Royal Oak in Lewes, and other events, having appeared at Sidmouth Festival in the 1990's. Now eighty-four, her voice is still strong and clear although she hasn't the range to reach the high notes as she did when younger.

Ken Stubbs met her and collected a number of songs from her in 1960 and it was under the name of Louey Saunders that she appeared on "Green Grow the Laurels" released by Topic records in 1976

Gordon Hall, Pease Pottage 1932 - 2000

Gordon Hall, one of the finest traditional singers of the late twentieth century, was a huge man both physically and in personality. He was blessed with a powerful and fine voice and in addition, had a great 'presence' which commanded respect.

Gordon's father was a cockney and his mother, Mabs, came from Wivelsfield in Sussex. They met and married when his father was invalided back from France during the Great War of 1914-18. They moved to Greenwich where Gordon was born in 1932, the second youngest of six children. After the start of the Second World War in 1939 his elder brothers were called up for military service and when the bombing of London started the family moved, first to Leeds, then to Swansea where his father worked in the docks. In 1942 when the blitz reached Wales the family moved to Horsham where they settled into a former home of the great folk singer Henry Burstow.

Gordon Hall *Jim Marshall*

Gordon was a star pupil at school but the family declined to accept a scholarship he won to Steyning Grammar School. He left school at fourteen to help his parents with a removal and coal business. In the early 50's he worked at Rusper brickworks and later for the gas company. Then, in the 1980's, he started working for a car breaker at Pease Pottage.

Gordon married in 1959 and had two children before his wife died suddenly in 1975. A few years later, in 1985 he moved to Pease Pottage near Crawley to live with his new partner Gill Lawrence until his death.

Gordon grew up in a talented musical family. His parents were both accomplished singers; his father favouring the Victorian music hall material and his mother the more 'traditional' country songs and ballads. Both his grandfather and great grandfather had been professional musicians with the Union Castle

Shipping Line, his grandfather rising from bandsman to musical director while his maternal grandmother was Irish with a wealth of old songs and stories. Inevitably there was always singing in the family, passing the old songs on from one generation to another. It was with some surprise that Gordon first encountered the folk song revival when he visited the 2-4-5 folk club in Crawley in the mid 80's and there he found other people who knew and sang songs similar to his own repertoire.

He now started to write down the vast store of songs from within the family and following early retirement began to research the four hundred or so songs attributed to Henry Burstow.

By now also the singing of both Gordon and his mother had been noted and they were invited to guest at both the National and Sidmouth Festivals as well as many folk clubs. Gordon however did not relish the festival scene and as time passed, although he would still accept an occasional club booking, his greatest pleasure was in the informal sessions such as the Sussex Singers night at the Ram, Firle.

A chain smoker for many years this, and fumes he inhaled in his the early days at the brickworks, eventually took their toll of his health and he died from cancer on 24 January 2000 aged sixty-seven.

The Veteran Tape VT131CD *"When the May is All in Bloom"* released in 1995 contains three tracks of Gordon and following his death, a full CD of Gordon produced by Jim Ward on Country Branch CD, CBCD095 *"Good Things Enough"* was released in 2000

The Coppers

No review of Sussex traditional singers would be complete without mention of the Coppers of Rottingdean. They are legendary far beyond their native Sussex and as the twentieth century ends are able to trace their family singing tradition back over 200 years to at least the eighteenth century while the earliest record of the family in the Parish Register is as far back as 1593

The family has a unique place in the history of the folk revival dating back to the last years of the nineteenth century when, unwittingly, they became a vital link in the creation of The Folk Song Society which was later to merge with the Dance Society to form the English Folk Dance and Song Society [E.F.D.S.S.].

In 1897 a certain Mrs Kate Lee was staying in the village of Rottingdean and heard of two local men renowned for their singing who were engaged in the running of a local farm and the Black Horse Inn. She invited both James 'Brasser' [1845-1924] and his younger brother Tom Copper to sing some old songs for her and was later to say *"I shall never forget the delight of hearing the two Mr Coppers..." "They were so proud of their Sussex songs and sang with an enthusiasm grand to hear...".* Carefully noting down what she heard she returned to London with some fifty songs and the following year, when she became involved in the creation of the Folk Song Society, published six of them in the Society's first Journal. This was to be the first organised move towards preserving the English song tradition and in due course both James and Tom Copper were made honorary founder members of the fledgling Society.

'Brasser's' two sons 'Jim' [James Dale] [1882-1954] and John [1879-1952] inherited a love of the old songs and maintained the family's singing tradition, passing it on, in due course, to their own sons Bob and Ron. In 1936 'Jim' wrote out the words of some sixty songs which had been passed down through the family by oral transmission for generations and today these still form the base of the family's repertoire.

Bob recalls that *"Grand-dad had died in 1924 but not before the spirit of singing the old songs, already adopted so faithfully by Jim and Uncle John, had been passed on to our generation. My cousin Ron and I sang together whenever the opportunity arose and also in a foursome with our fathers. Ron took on the base line with Jim while I modelled my style on and sang with Uncle John. Right up until the nineteen-thirties the Black Horse was still the place for a sing-song on a Saturday night ...."*

In 1950 Jim Copper heard a version of one of their songs sung on the BBC's Country Life programme and at Bob's insistence wrote to the Corporation to say how pleased he had been to hear one of his family's songs sung on the radio. The BBC quickly visited the family and made a number of recordings. Later that year the family made their first radio broadcast and many of their songs were noted for the BBC musical archives. This led to the BBC embarking on fieldwork to collect and preserve traditional songs from practically every county in the British Isles and was to lead to the folk revival in Britain.

Bob Copper *[left]*
and
Ron Copper *[right]*
Bob Copper

In January 1952 they were invited to sing at the English Folk Dance and Song Society's annual two-day festival at the Royal Albert Hall in London. The following day the music critic of The Star wrote, *"Surprise of the Folk*

189

Dance Festival at the Albert Hall was the traditional folk song singing by four of a Rottingdean family. John Copper, 73; his brother James, 70; and their respective sons Ronald, 40 and Robert, 36.
It was the first stage appearance of these Sussex characters from the B.B.C.'s 'Country Magazine'. They came in their work-a-day clothes and spurning a microphone sang 'Brisk and Bonny Lad' and 'Twanky Dillo' naturally and sweetly. Their words, unlike those of many professional singers, were clear and comprehensible."

All four were made honorary members of the English Folk Dance and Song Society repeating the awarded made over fifty years earlier to 'Brasser' and Tom Copper.

For more details of the family's background and songs see 'A Song For Every Season' a hundred years of a Sussex farming family by Bob Copper published 1971 by William Heinemann Ltd.

Ron Copper, Rottingdean 1912 - 1978

Son of John Copper, Ron was born in Rottingdean on 2 September 1912 and died there on 7 January 1978 at the age of sixty-five. He was for many years landlord of the Queen Victoria. Ron was renowned for his rich bass voice, which, for many, gave the Coppers such a distinctive sound through the early years of the folk revival.

Eddie Upton wrote an obituary in the Folk Diary No.50 "The name of the Copper family is well-known to anyone remotely interested in English traditional singing. The Coppers have lived in the Rottingdean area for over three hundred years and for much of that time have been singing the songs of the village. They developed their own style of harmony singing and it's thanks to Ron and his cousin Bob that we have been able to hear the songs as they were sung to the folksong collectors of the nineteenth century. Many have tried to copy them, but nobody has been able to emulate the rich deep resonance of Ron's bass voice.
Anyone who met Ron will testify to the great love that he had for his songs. I was fortunate to have met him many years ago, soon after I became interested in folk song. Ron was always happy to meet people who were interested in his music. He was especially pleased when young people took up the tradition.
He was essentially a very unassuming man. He did not seem to be aware that for many people he was a notable figure in the folk music world. I recall a group of us spending evenings with him in his pub, talking to him and trying to get him to sing. He was delighted to talk, but he was always more interested in hearing us sing and joining in with us. Many will remember him coming to Bob's club and standing quietly at the back, listening to other people's songs.

Ron had suffered from ill-health for some time so his public appearances over the last few months were severely limited. However, he was well enough to appear at last year's Brighton Folk Festival. The singing of the Copper family was the highlight of the festival. It was a delight to sit in the room listening to them and watching a hard-bitten music critic beside himself with pleasure at their singing. Fortunately, the BBC were there to record the occasion.

It is a sad task to write an obituary for Ron Copper, but it is a lasting joy to have known him and heard him singing."

Robert 'Bob' James Copper, Peacehaven 1915 -

Bob was born in Rottingdean on 6 January 1915 the son of Jim Copper. It was there that he went to school and in 1929 left to become a 'lather-boy' at the local barbershop. In 1933 he joined the Life Guards as a trooper and from 1936 to 47 was a detective constable with the West Sussex Constabulary. After that he took over a licensed social club in Peacehaven where, with the exception of two years as mine host at a pub in Cheriton Hampshire, he remained until handing the club over to his son John.

Bob Copper at Seaford Folk Club, September 1998 *the author*

During the 1950's he worked for the BBC collecting songs, music and dialect from Sussex and Hampshire and some years later memories of both his life in and around Rottingdean and the time spent collecting were put to good use when he assumed the mantle of author. In 1971 he was awarded the Robert Pitman Literary Prize for his first book 'A Song for Every Season', mentioned earlier. This was followed by two further volumes 'Songs and Southern Breezes' in 1973 and 'Early to Rise' in 1976 In the 1990's he was again busy writing with two books 'Across Sussex with Belloc' and 'Bob Copper's Sussex'.

In February 2000, at the age of eighty-five, he was presented with an honorary degree of Master of Arts by Sussex University for services to country life. This included the collecting and singing of traditional songs as well as his writings.

Today the family tradition is maintained. Bob, now eighty-seven, continues to perform both solo and with the family group. In 1965 Bob's son John, on his sixteenth birthday, sang with his father at the Albert Hall in a concert called 'Sounds of Folk'. Later his daughter Jill became part of the group, followed sometime after Ron's death, by her partner John Dudley – one of the organisers of the early Seaford folk clubs. Within the past few months John's three children Ben, Lucy and Tom together with Jill's three, Mark, Andy and Sean Barratt have also started singing, making them at least the seventh consecutive generation of the family to sing their own established repertoire reaching back to the eighteenth century.

The song clubs, even the singers, come and go but the songs; they go on forever.

INDEX

INDIVIDUALS:

193

194

MANZEL, Nigel: 54, 97

MASTERSON, Terry: 39, **39**, 41, 49, 55, 69, **69**, 76, **76**, 81, 88, 89, **89**, 90, **91**, 93, 94, 97, 98, 114, 123, 129, 130, 132, 134, 138, 139, 146, 149, 151, 154-156, **155**, 157, 163, 165, 168

MATTHEWS, Brian: 17, **18**, 19, 166, **166**, 170, 172, 174, 178

MAYNARD, George 'Pop': 8, **8**, 17, 166, 169, 170, **171**, 171-172

McCLUSKEY, John 'Kluggers': 66, **66**, 67

McDONALD, 'Whispering' Bob: 20, 25, 27, **28**, 29, 38, 39, 74, **75**, 77, 79, 80, **80**, 104, 113

MacMAHON, Frank: 69, **69**

McRORY-WILSON, Mike: 69, 155

MEADOWS, Eric: 62, **63**, 64, 105, 167

MEDDINGS, Keith and Cherry: 57

MESSAGE, Kelvin: 87, **87,** 88

MIDDLETON, Dave: 98, 117

MILLER, Andy: **126**

MORGAN, Don: 44, **49**, 57, 77, **77**, 81, 90

MORGAN, Sarah: 44, **49**, 57, 77, **77**, 81

MORRIS, Paul: 9, **75**

MORRISON, Grace: 101, **102**

MOUSDELL, Harry: 10, 11, 12, 78, 110, **110**, 126, 143, 145, 176, 177

MURREN, Don: 105

MURRAY, Alan: 35, **36**

NASH, Roy: 13, 98, 110, **110**

NEVILL, Steve: 101, **102**

NEVILLE, Eric: 46, **47**

NICHOLSON, Lea: 54, **55**, 62, 81, 104, 125, 139, 153

NORSWORTHY, Mary [see APPS, Mary]

OAKLEY, George: 98, 139

O'GORMAN, Lynn [see WATTS, Lynn]

OLIVER, Charlotte: 44, **44**, 139

O'REAGAN-KING, Ainneagh: 71

O'ROURKE, Sean: 88

ORCHIN, Mark: 103

PHILLIPS, Cyril: 10, 41, **41**, 105, 107, 137, 141, 170, **180**, 180-181

PICKARD, Ivor: 34, **35**, 37, 81, **136**

POPE, Ron: 44, 45, 81, 84, **85**

POTTER, Terry: 10, 11, 13, 59, 138, 144

PRICE, Jenn: 50, **107**

PUMP and PLUCK BAND: 106, **107**, 134, 141, 144, 168

QUINN, Dan: 99, **100**

RAWLINSON, Paul: 87

REED, Stuart: 34, 58, **59**, 60, **60**, 61, 63, 65, 69, 105, 126, 134, 141

RICHARDSON, Dick: 9, 11, 12, 19, 25, **25**, 29, 38, 139, 172

ROGERS, Mike: 38

ROSE, Geoff and Shirley: 11, 20, 25, **25**

ROSE, Hazel: 101, **102**, 117

RUFFELL, Barry: 44

SAWDY, Mavis: 44

SCARLETT, Terry: **11**, 14, 15, 16, 19, 20, **21**, 22, 25, **25**, 26, 74, 75, **75**, 79, 113, 167

SETFORD, Paul: 34, 39, **40**, 44, 73, 78, **79**, 81, 113, 122, 123, 130, 134, 135, 143, 154, 156-158, **157**, 177

SHOUGH, Indrani: 64, 65, **65**, 105

SHOUGH, Martin: 64, 65, **65**, 121

SMITH, Lesley: 64, **64**, 65, 85

SMITH, Tina: 54, **55**, 56, 71, 81, 89, **89**, 91, 93, 94, **94**, 95, **95**, 96, 99, **99**, 105, 106, 116, 118, **118**, 122, 126, 131, 132, 135, 136, **136**, 138, 139, 140, 149, 151-154, **152**, **153**, 155, 168

SMITH, Vic: 34, 37, 49, 53, 54, 55, **55**, 56, 57, 59, 60, 61, 67, 71, 73, 81, 89, **89**, 90, **91**, 93, 94, **94**, 95, **95**, 96, 99, **99**, 100, 103, 104, 105, 106, 108, 116, 118, **118**, 119, **119**, 121, 122, 123, 125, 126, **126**, 131, 132, 133, 135, 136, **136**, 137, 138, 139, 140, 144, 149, 151-154, **152**, **154**, 157, 160, 163, 168, 170, 177, 178, 179

196

THE CLUBS: